Harriet Stuart

ℒ♥

A FEW

THOUSAND WORDS

ABOUT LOVE

ℒ♥

ALSO BY MICKEY PEARLMAN

AUTHOR

WHAT TO READ: The Essential Guide for Reading Group Members and Other Book Lovers

LISTEN TO THEIR VOICES: Twenty Interviews with Women Who Write

COAUTHOR

A VOICE OF ONE'S OWN: Conversations with America's Writing Women (with Katherine Usher Henderson)

TILLIE OLSEN (with Abby H. P. Werlock)

EDITOR

AMERICAN WOMEN WRITING FICTION: Memory, Identity, Family, Space

MOTHER PUZZLES: Daughters and Mothers in Contemporary American Literature

THE ANNA BOOK: Searching for Anna in Literary History

CANADIAN WOMEN WRITING FICTION

BETWEEN FRIENDS: Writing Women Celebrate Friendship

A PLACE CALLED HOME: Twenty Writing Women Remember

ST. MARTIN'S PRESS

NEW YORK

A FEW

THOUSAND WORDS

ABOUT LOVE

EDITED BY
MICKEY PEARLMAN

A FEW THOUSAND WORDS ABOUT LOVE
Copyright © Mickey Pearlman, 1998
All rights reserved. Printed in the United States of America. No part of this
book my be used or reproduced in any manner whatsoever without written
permission except in the case of brief quotations embodied in critical articles
or reviews. For information, address St. Martin's Press, Scholarly and
Reference Division, 175 Fifth Avenue, New York, N.Y. 10010

Brian Hall's "Mortal Love" is reprinted by permission of the author from
Madeleine's World, Houghton Mifflin, 1997.

Peter Cameron's "Excerpts from Swan Lake" was originally published in *The
Half You Don't Know: Selected Stories,* NAL/Dutton, 1997.

Joyce Carol Oates' "First Love" © The Ontario Review, Inc.

ISBN 0-312-17355-5

Library of Congress Cataloging-in-Publication Data

A few thousand words about love/Mickey Pearlman.
        p.   cm.
   Includes bibliographical references and index.
   ISBN 0-312-17355-5
   1. Love. 2. Interperonal attraction. 3. Man-woman
   relationships. 4. Interpersonal relations. I. Pearlman, Mickey.
HM132.F48   1998
306.7—dc21   97-41490
                                                                CIP

First St. Martin's edition: January, 1998
10 9 8 7 6 5 4 3 2 1

FOR MARV:

love object

AND IN MEMORY OF DEENA STUTMAN
(1943 – 1996),

who believed in the possibility of goodness,
and the goodness of possibility.

CONTENTS

ACKNOWLEDGMENTS

You can't do it alone, that's for sure, so thanks to the following workerpeople, all of whom are also funny, smart and kind: Vicky Bijur (agent), Michael Flamini (editor), Meredith Howard (publicist), and Alan Bradshaw (production).

Thanks too for the empowering and continuing friendship of the ABC Sandys (Appleman, Benítez, Cohen), and to Jill Shanker and Arlene Hirschfelder.

—M.P.

✒

A FEW

THOUSAND WORDS

ABOUT LOVE

✒

PREFACE

A Few Thousand Words about Love is about people. To be precise, it is about those people we love and have loved: grandmothers, including one who had an affair with George Gershwin (by Katharine Weber), and the loveable but confused character created by Peter Cameron in a short story. It is about children—and about adoption and childbirth, sibling rivalry and sonograms (Brian Hall, Myra Goldberg, Dennis McFarland, Caroline Leavitt, and Ron Carlson), and grown-up daughters (Carolyn See). It is, even in this age of cynicism, about love affairs (Larry O'Connor, Ron Carlson, Shawn Wong, and Dennis McFarland), and it seems striking and somehow comforting to this editor of the female gender that the most liltingly "romantic" essays were not only written by men, but about their wives. (Cynics, postmodernists, and angstlovers lament!)

On the other hand, Joyce Carol Oates's contribution is a fiction/memoir about a young white woman's obsession with a young black man, and Linda Hogan's poem is about good old-fashioned passion! And the women had their own love affairs to talk about: with characters in movies (Elizabeth McCracken), and in books (Angela Davis-Gardner), and with the country that contains us all (Margot Livesey).

1

Of course, love has many objects, some of them the "uncles," "aunts," neighbors, and friends who *function* as family—the kind you *want* to show up at Thanksgiving, and Tim Gautreaux, Angela Davis-Gardner, and I, among others, wrote about them.

It's impossible, of course, (but always enticing) to try to make some viable observations that will hold up, hold water, and be helpful to the reader. It's always dangerous (since this is where the critics start to lick their chops)—but here goes. The women are funnier: Elizabeth McCracken on Abbott and Costello, Carolyn See on ex-husbands, Margot Livesey on unfamiliar sex acts behind potted palms, Katharine Weber on coffee grinds and toes. Caroline Leavitt even finds some humor in the intricate details of an unexpected and nearly fatal childbirth experience, and Myra Goldberg makes you laugh at head lice and bigotry—both of which make an appearance in her essay about her daughter, Anna.

The men, on the other hand, write often about longing and the wonderful intimacy that exists between well-matched lovers and between well-loved children and their parents. In the world of this collection, at least, men are diapering, babysitting, washing dishes, and looking back to childhoods in the mossy bayous of southern Louisiana and the fishing camps of Utah.

No wifebeating, no child abuse, no emasculating wives, no serial killers. Reading *A Few Thousand Words about Love* might even, at least temporarily, bring back optimism. Which is, after all, what defines *love.*

—MICKEY PEARLMAN

2

LONGEVITY

RON CARLSON

I'VE BEEN MARRIED more than twenty-eight years, and what men do at this juncture is give their wives credit for the *longevity* of their marriages, using that word, *longevity,* which is a word for the ages though not particularly a personal or joyous or appropriate word, certainly not a word to be used in private, say over a glass of wine in the kitchen late at night, "Thank you, my dear, for the longevity..." or in the tangled bed, unless it might be ventured as a joke, but then who would say it?

We were twenty-one and twenty-two the year we wed, and through the years we've been able to move through the many rooms of this marriage, which primarily means my wife was strong and forgiving while I finally matured. It takes forever in this country, because we don't champion maturity. It, after all, is the enemy of the marketplace, the economy. We make a point of celebrating want here, elevating it to need, and every film, song, and book is intended to be part of the ubiquitous machinery that sends us once again to the store. I finally realized I was mature this year because I hadn't been in a store, other than the grocery, for fifteen months; that's the only test we've got left, the only rite. You stay out of the mall long enough to let the snow melt and you've made it. I don't want to get side-tracked into that entire discussion about marketeers targeting everybody age 18 to 34, because they are sure those people are immature, and how now that group has become 18 to 49, because there's a real good chance you can find the empty space in those folks too, nobody quite finished, grown up, but that discussion—maturity in America—is absolutely related, shot through any discussion of sustained love. It is not by mistake that all the great love songs of former eras take easy reincarnation as advertisement soundtracks; a broken heart is about need, and longing, well, that is always longing. What we should be after is the way to turn longing into longevity. Is there a chance of that? The reason I've been married this long and will be married for the whole deal is—yes, in fact partly because my wife Elaine is utterly resourceful and large-hearted—but the part of the credit I will take is simply this: I never imagined anything else. I actively imagined this. Even at times when I was right against the broken window of rocky times, I never saw anything but this, a marriage, and all the dear and trying vicissitudes of that terrific and muscular and vivid and intimate word: *longevity*.

THE FIRST PHOTOGRAPH of me after our wedding was taken in Urie, Wyoming, and I am standing next to a buffalo. It was the first full day of my marriage, and the photograph I'm speaking of was taken by my new bride, Elaine Craig, whose new name was Elaine Carlson, and who had taken my name the day before at the First Congregational Church in Salt Lake City, Utah. Elaine and I were headed east toward our first teaching jobs in a place we'd never been (Connecticut!), and we were very serious and not totally easy with each other, already out of state, as they say, but we'd decided to make this one side trip south of Interstate 80 to see if the buffalo were still there at the old Thunderbird Oil station in Urie. The stretch of highway from Evanston, Wyoming, east to Fort Bridger was full of memories for me because it was the way my father had taken our family fishing dozens of times to the Uinta Mountains when I was a boy.

I could see the snowcapped Uintas, the only mountain range in the country that runs east and west, as I posed for the picture. The old bull buffalo was grazing near the fence, which was nothing but a single loopy strand of barbed wire. I stepped up the grassy bank to this fence and stood shoulder to shoulder with the beast. Elaine, still back at the car, snapped the photograph. It's a good picture, as you can imagine. There I am, a kid in his wedding suit, tie and all for some reason, the day after we were wed, and as I reached to touch his horn, the buffalo turned his massive head suddenly and lipped the carnation from my suitcoat, knocking me into the ditch. This isn't fiction. Buffaloes are big, and I know for a fact that they'll eat flowers.

What a trip. That night we'd stay in a motel in Cheyenne, Wyoming. Twelve dollars it cost. The next night we'd be in Atlantic, Iowa, and stay on the third floor of the Boss Whitney hotel. Maybe you've been there. Then Benton Harbor, Michigan, in a Hilton. It was so expensive, but lovely, and I remember being embarrassed talking to my parents on the telephone as Elaine came out of the shower wrapped in a towel. Hi, Mom, hi, Dad, here's Elaine, she's naked.

What a honeymoon, really; we were innocent enough to have invented the continent. We ended up the next night in Buffalo, New York, and it was like this. I was looking through some pamphlets on the bureau in our motel when I said to Elaine: Hey, do you know what's here? Neither of us knew. Niagara Falls! I'm not kidding; look on the map. We went to Niagara Falls on our honeymoon—no wonder the marriage took. It was 1969 and they had shut off the American side for repairs. They were going to shore up the lip to prevent further erosion. Even with half of it shut off, the one dry cliff dripping in the daylight, Niagara Falls was big. I remember reading in the paper that when they dried up the American side, they found two old cars and a body.

TEN YEARS LATER to the date, the exact date, and that's how ten years passes, by saying the word "later," we were on the Isle of Skye off the western coast of Scotland, and the photographer Elaine Carlson was at it again. This second photo was taken at about ten o'clock at night, though there was still plenty of the heady northern twilight. It wasn't dark. The photo shows me standing on the road in front of the pub in Bradford. I'm all wet and grinning like a kid, a fishing pole in one hand, and above my shoulder in Bradford Harbor you can barely see a submarine. This is the only known photograph of Ron Carlson and a submarine. It was our tenth anniversary.

We'd spent a crazy, rainy day on the train, coming across the top of Scotland, drinking ale and staring out the window at the peatbogs, green-gray, and trying to read. The train was nearly empty and we played Gin, but it was not any good playing Gin. It's been a marriage where we've played Gin on and off all the years—saving thousands and thousands of dollars in counselor's fees by playing in the bathtub during one tough, and I mean tough (this is nonfiction), winter, and Elaine has the knack; it's instinct really. She got it from her father, and she can win; she can lay a card face down on the discard pile before I've got my clubs arranged. On the train, weary of reading and dull to Gin, we made up games: first "phone numbers." You cite the number and the other person has to tell you what it's for. It would be easy, even at this remove, to remember the names of the friends we invoked; they're still our friends—isn't that strange?

Then, of course, the game degenerated to the point where one of us (I'll say in the spirit of true nonfiction that it was probably me) would offer up a number that meant nothing to either of us, such as the number from Brothers' Pizza, which I had memorized from the box, along with everything else: the goofy chef, so happy to be there, circling thumb and first finger to show how perfect things were. We were a long way from home on a train.

Why do I remember that day almost twenty years ago now so well? The two of us, married to the bones, sick of travel, finally staring at each other like siblings. I made up the final game: Face Tennis. Like all couples, we had our way of speaking, of grooming each other like monkeys: "Honey, there's something on your face, by your mouth (here), in your nose." So that day on the train we played Face Tennis: your eyebrows need plucking; your lips are chapped; there's something in the corner of your eye; did you wash your hair? We went back and forth until the volley was dropped. I think we played one point of that nasty game until we pulled apart and sulked, both insulted in the corner of Scotland, headed for land's end.

Immediately after stowing our stuff at the tiny bed and breakfast we'd found at the end of the little road headed west out of Bradford, I'd ducked out and gone fishing. We needed to be apart, and being a boy, I needed to be outside. The bay was rocky and promising, and as I picked my way out across the rocky lea, I realized I'd never thrown a lure east into the sea before. It was a large Scottish evening, great clashing shipments of clouds crossing the sun until the day went under and I reeled in for the last time. It was an odd moment for me on that slippery outcropping. Listen to this. I turned around and found myself cut off from the island by the tide that had now risen four feet. Well, I'm not an islander. I'm a guy from Utah. We have different tides. It was almost dark there on the Isle of Skye (and the lesser isle, on which I trembled). I had a lot of thoughts, none of them any help. Is the water still rising? How much longer will it rise? How deep is it now? How cold is it? Is it shark-infested? Is it in any way infested? When they find my body, how will it look?

The last was the best thought, most characteristic of the drama boys love, the melodrama that walks at the edges of my life. But it—

along with all the others—was overwhelmed by an impulse to get back across the forty yards of ocean that had opened between me and the island on which my wife was mad at me for having insulted her on a train, and I plunged into the North Sea and found it two and three and then four feet deep and real cold, and then five feet like fear and then over my head as I tripped in the ocean and scrambled and found rock and footing and then dry ground on which to sputter and proclaim once again. So much for Toiler of the Sea. Wet to my eyeballs, I sloshed up into town and into the pub where I found Elaine, dry and toasty, having a pint of Guinness with a young American who was staying down the road in a hostel. Even soaking wet, it is possible to enjoy a couple pints of bitter, which I did, cheered by survival and my young wife's concern. An hour later, we walked out into the lingering evening and paused on the path so a woman could photograph her wet, grinning husband before going up to our bed and breakfast. There we found our host and hostess ready with tea and cookies. They had a purebred chocolate Labrador, a lustrous animal who would sit motionless with a cookie on his nose until the master signaled for him to flip the wafer up and catch it in his mouth. It was our tenth anniversary, and we had conversation and dog tricks for an hour and all the cookies were gone. It was a small house and our room had twin beds, and in the spirit of true nonfiction, I'll say it was Elaine who slipped into my bed where side by side we were very quiet.

That year in Europe the only time we hitchhiked was in Wales, headed for Laugharne. There was no train south from the main line and some of the buses had names a quarter mile long. We held our thumbs out in the rain, and a moment later had a ride with a muscular bloke in a two-door Ford full of cigarette smoke. When he found out we were Yanks, he started an encomium of John Wayne, who had died that spring, and before we knew it, the driver was crying, wiping tears with his beefy hands and saying he'd drive us all the way down to Laugharne even if it was ten kilometers out of his way.

We were disaffected with John Wayne at the time. He had been making strident pro-Vietnam noises for five years and that had over-shadowed *Stagecoach* and all the rest. His attitude toward the war in Southeast Asia and toward the students and activists who had op-posed it had canceled our sympathies for him. This big, weeping Welshman gave us pause. We'd give John Wayne one more chance, I was sure; in fact later I'd put him in a story. But not in this chapter of our lives. This is the "couple in Europe" chapter, not the "trying to have kids chapter." A marriage with staying power, ten rooms and a view, longing and longevity, has room for John Wayne.

Years before, my lottery number for the Selective Service System military draft had been 111, and if I had been called, I would have gone to Vietnam. For a while I thought I was safe because I had registered in Houston and my draft board was large, but in the spring of 1970 I was summoned for my draft physical. Elaine and I stayed up most of the night talking and just before noon the next day I sat in a wooden chair in my jockey shorts while a doctor held my foot in his hand and examined the contours of the bunions on the side. "You can get dressed," he said, and I remember his exact words: "We're not making boots for you." I ran all the way home and when I came through the door with flowers I couldn't afford, four hours early, Elaine's face blanched. She thought I was being shipped that afternoon. Unlike three million others, we had been spared.

AFTER OUR CAR ride in Wales that rainy afternoon, we walked down the path past Dylan Thomas's writing studio, that famous little room, to the gate of his house in Laugharne, which was then a museum during the daytime hours curated by a vivacious woman named Vicky Wiggins. She greeted us and showed us the living quarters on the second floor, a kind of dorm arrangement for visiting school groups. That evening after everyone had left, Elaine and I had free range of the place, and I sat on the estuary wall and fished, flinging my gallant lure into the churning waters. In the morning when we awoke the entire bay would be drained, the tide leaving a shiny, veined mud flat. These fluctuating waters were out to trick me.

That night we went down to the Three Mariners, the pub we'd read about for years, on the corner in the village, and where, that year, the original proprietors were still in charge. The gentleman had had a stroke and sat to one side while his seventy-year-old wife tended bar. "Dylan Thomas," she said to our obvious question. "Yes, oh yes, we knew him. And if he acted the way they say he did when he was in America, then I'm ashamed of him."

On the way home, Elaine was stricken suddenly with the urgent need to relieve her bladder and ducked into some bushes which turned out to be some kind of Welsh stinging nettle that gave her a brilliant rash. The rash, we found out that year in Wales, was communicable. Sprawled on a lower bunk, I began to itch and laugh at the same time. It's a good word for a marriage: *communicable.*

COMMUNICATION. FIVE YEARS later, alone in Sun Valley close to eleven P.M., the temperature ten below zero, I hung up the phone in the convenience store at the top of the town and the clerk saw my face. It had been too cold to use the phone outside, and I stood in the back leaning against a stack of beer cases. "Are you all right?" he asked. It was kind of him really, some kid who wanted his customers to come in and buy a six of Coke and cigarettes and not to cry, but his question helped me make it across the frozen street to the Blue Tops, where I was staying those awful days. Tough times, we say, bad little eras in a marriage, the times for which there are no photographs, but to leave them out would be wrong. How many mistakes are we capable of? Plenty. How many do I take as my share? That night, that walk home through a cold that wanted to kill me, and my heart which would have let it, informs the word *longevity*, as much as any in our history. If the rope holds in the thin dark places, then it will hold.

IMAGINATION IS A powerful navigator, and all my days I have actively imagined living with one woman, and I developed the custom of not imagining other things. Let me say this again: when circumstance and mistake forced me to the brink from where it is utterly possible to imagine other things, I couldn't. I already had one thing I was imagining and there was no room for any other. I do believe, as a writer and as a citizen of this larger world, we get the things we imagine.

And as for living a life with one woman, that's an intriguing illusion, because in a long marriage, you live with many; and they must suffer many of you. I don't know how that explains the fact that the two of you end up looking like each other, but it must be evolutionary, some quiet, intractable survival trait.

WE'RE JUST NOW finishing a chapter that would be best called "Elaine in her Boyhood." She was the middle of three sisters and having two sons has been something she jumped into with both feet. Of all the activities and sports she's mastered as part of this long-term program, the most notorious episode occurred with her cub scout troop. Leading her five scouts (including her two sons), she did the Pinewood Derby; she did the crafts and the camping; she did the skits. I can't describe the relish with which she entered these things. Then the day her group was to cook pizza in a cardboard oven, there was a fire. They'd cooked the pizza and were enjoying it out in the yard and discussing the lessons learned, when the superheated box burst brightly into flame and everyone jumped up, alarmed. One of her eager charges yelled, "Stop! Drop! And roll!" Before anyone could do that, Elaine made her reputation by kicking the entire deal into our inground spa. As the charcoaled box hissed and sank, the scouts gathered round, one kid saying, "Cool."

The moments I cherish are those in the bed when we've put the books down and she's recounting something like that, laughing, saying it: "Stop! Drop! And roll." I remember as a boy hearing my parents laughing in the bedroom, and I feel as lucky as any person to have such a thing in my life.

Let's go back, though, to Tokyo, and an important reunion. She'd been there three months editing computer manuals for Mitsubishi and Sperry. Oh, to see someone again. In the back of the cab we fell together and kissed. It was dark on the island of Honshu and the lights of Tokyo rose in shimmering echelons on the windshield, and fresh from the plane my own sense of time was a simmering flicker in my forehead. We had each other back again. What we didn't know was: a little baby boy who would be our son Nicholas lay in a crib in an orphanage in Santa Anna, fifty miles north of the capital of El Salvador. He was ten weeks old. And in an unnamed Utah town a young woman we didn't know had missed her period three weeks before, and in a month she would make a hard decision. The next year we would stand awkwardly in our kitchen while our lawyer's wife, crying fully, and whispering through it, "He's so beautiful," would hand Elaine our youngest son, Colin. Six weeks later his brother Nick would fly in from El Salvador, eleven months old, and I would buy every cigar in the Salt Lake City International Airport gift shop. I mean, it was Utah; there weren't that many. We'd gone from no children to two in six weeks; younger child first.

We kissed there in the immaculate back seat of that taxi. Breaking for air in bliss and fatigue, I would see the driver turn and waggle his first finger at the two Americans in the back seat. What had he said? *Not in Japan.* I'm not making this up. This is nonfiction; useful information you can take away. Don't start kissing in the back of a cab in Japan. You're going to get scolded, which depending on your state of mind and the hour of the day can be kind of refreshing.

AND WHAT ABOUT this parental decision? Three years later we're sitting in our Arizona kitchen drinking cheap cold beer and playing Gin. We're trying to decide what to tell the boys. Not about adoption. They know all about that; that's a good deal. At preschool, all of Nick's classmates were born in Mesa, Arizona; he gets a lot of mileage out of El Salvador. We're having trouble deciding when to tell the kids that dinosaurs and men did not live during the same epochs. And you can judge us as harshly as you like. We try hard as parents and primarily it's a joy, living with these two guys, the funniest two people either of us has ever known, and really our major stake in the future, but we decided after ten hands and a six-pack not to tell them.

We grow up. If we're lucky, which means simply blessed by the jillion coincidences a big world affords, and we pay attention more often than not because our hearts require it—life is such a manifold curiosity!—then we wake almost thirty years after I climbed out of a ditch in Urie, Wyoming and walked toward Elaine who is laughing by the car. I remember that day and most of what has happened since. We'd been married almost one day. It seemed to have a certain longevity. We would spend that night in a motel in Cheyenne. I remember lying on the bed in my pajama bottoms, something you wear on a honeymoon, reading a book we'd been given as a wedding present, a paperback copy of *The Days of Dylan Thomas*. It was full of pictures of his beautiful wife Caitlin and their beautiful house in Laugharne. Our plan was to go there someday. I heard the bathroom door open and looked up to see Elaine in a sleeveless white nightgown, something you wear on a honeymoon, something they make so you can mostly see through it. Elaine came to bed. This was over ten thousand nights ago, and as I felt the bed move that night, our second, I had a thought, an irrevocable thought about the irrevocable nature of certain things. "You're married now, Ron Carlson," I thought then. This is not fiction, this is historical fact here. "This looks a lot like marriage."

THE MEMORY OF ALL THAT

KATHARINE WEBER

WHEN I STARTED spending time with the man who would be my husband, I began to notice a strong and pleasing odor of coffee wafting up from his feet. Not only did his shoes smell good, they also occasionally contained a few grains of actual coffee grounds. This was, I soon discovered, the consequence of Nick having purchased an enormous and ancient coffee grinder from a defunct A&P in Vermont for eight dollars. In his tiny makeshift cabin on the edge of a forest in northern Connecticut there was only one outlet wired seriously enough not to blow all the fuses every time he ground coffee, and it was in the back of his only closet.

How could I not fall in love with a man whose feet smelled of freshly ground coffee?

COFFEE WAS—if not mother's milk—grandmother's milk to me. My grandmother drank coffee habitually. A lipstick-printed coffee cup makes me think of her still. The smell of stewed coffee (not the brilliant notes of Starbucks single estate roasts, but the muddy chords of coffee shop java) can still take me right back to my grandmother's coffee table. It was, literally, a coffee table, and when I was a child it was just the right height for me. I would linger at the serving tray until I was given permission to select one—just one—sugar lump, which I was then permitted to dip into my grandmother's black coffee.

In the living room of my grandmother's New York apartment, the aroma of coffee permeated the rippling scales of grown-up laughter, the jangle of her bracelets as she removed them, and the resonance of piano music as felt from my vantage point on the rug under the baby grand, where I could keep a close eye on her beautiful shoes as they moved over the pedals.

My grandmother played songs about love; some of them she had written herself. Mostly the music was witty and upbeat, but there were also slow, sad songs of loss. Curled under the piano, watching an elegant foot tap perfect time, I would weep discreetly, moved in ways I didn't understand by the words and music. Something about the songs, and my grandmother playing and singing in her high voice, and my mother sitting on the couch listening and occasionally singing along in a lower octave, made those moments seem, somehow, profoundly about the secret essence of life.

The coffee cut the sweetness of the sugar. There was an art to wicking up maximum coffee without letting the lump dissolve in my fingers. It was all in the timing.

WHEN I WAS a child, I heard the name George Gershwin invoked with such frequency and fond familiarity that I concluded he was a very close relative. I knew he was dead, but I assumed that his death was a fairly recent event, as he was still referred to with contemporary intimacy by members of my family.

The way he came into my consciousness wasn't only because of the music, but the music was always there. One of my earliest memories consists of being pushed in a supermarket cart, my bare legs dangling down through those wire openings in the chromed mesh that left grooves on the backs of my thighs. The syrupy tune wafting in the air comes to an end, and a new melody begins. My mother, whose shopping list and pocketbook I hold, cocks her head in a particular focused way and leans down, murmuring to me, "That's George." Inevitably, I developed a precocious ability to recognize Gershwin tunes everywhere. By the age of seven, I could name that tune in four or five notes. It occurs to me now that the skill I had acquired was not, in fact, the ability to recognize Gershwin music, though that certainly came with time. My primary expertise was a highly attuned ability to recognize the look on my mother's face and take it as a cue to pipe up, "That's George!" In this way I could join my mother in her secret pleasure.

What was the pleasure, exactly? I was never sure. I knew she had been very close to him as a child; perhaps the music brought back those pleasant times. Maybe these little moments gave us a sense of superiority over all the ordinary people around us who had no idea what they were hearing, who had no Gershwin connection, as they wandered the aisles of the A&P on Metropolitan Avenue. I felt proprietary about George's music, the way my mother did, and loved by it the way my mother had felt loved by him—and so I loved the music back.

George was everywhere. "That dog looks just like George's dog Tony," my mother would remark, spotting a scruffy terrier on a street in our Forest Hills neighborhood.

"Never part your hair on the right, always on the left," my grandmother would admonish me; "George always told me to part my hair on the left because it showed my sense of humor."

THERE WERE SEVERAL inscribed photographs of George (as I, too, thought of him) around my grandmother's 59th Street apartment. Each time I visited her, after gazing out the window at the lacy girders of the Queensboro Bridge, playing with her miniature music boxes, examining all the little glass and silver treasures on her mantlepiece, and studying various family pictures, I would go from room to room (the ritual aspect of my devotions unnoticed by any adult) and pay a call on each of the photographs of George.

Who did I think he was? When I was very little, I wasn't quite sure exactly how George fit in. Somehow I knew that my grandmother, Ganz, had loved him, that the songs were about the two of them. (All the grandchildren called her Ganz, a nickname developed out of a cute mispronunciation when my oldest cousin, the first grandchild, was a baby. Ganz suited her far better than anything "grandma"- or "nanna"-ish ever could have. My own children called her Ganz. My husband called her Ganz.)

Ganz had loved George, and then he had died all of a sudden. She rarely mentioned her first husband, my grandfather, though I saw him and his young wife (who was my mother's age) and their children (who were my age) two or three times a year. They were "real" family, but Ganz's preference for George over the elderly man called Pop seemed reasonable to me: my grandfather was old and wrinkled, while George had been young and smooth.

By the time I was a little older I understood much more. My grandfather, too, I realized, had once been young and smooth—very handsome, in fact—but for some reason, as if the words to all the songs I knew so well were literally about them, Ganz had fallen in love with George and they had, for ten years—for the last ten years of my grandparents' marriage—carried on a romance. A love affair.

"They had an affair," my mother had replied bluntly, provoked by my asking, reasonably, hopefully, if Ganz hadn't perhaps been married to George. She seemed so much like his widow, despite the two subsequent husbands. I was disappointed at the realization that whatever he was to us, there was no tidy name for it. (And I wondered too, after my mother uttered the word "affair" for the first time, what it had to do with a certain sign out in front of a tacky restaurant on Queens Boulevard that read, "Have Your Next Affair With Us!")

Being a methodical child, I looked the word up in the dictionary. An affair was "a concern, a business, a matter to be attended to, a celebrated or notorious or noteworthy happening or sequence of events." I knew all that already, but what did it mean?

WHEN I WAS in second grade, I asked the music enrichment teacher (obnoxiously, I'm sure) if she had ever heard of George Gershwin. Encouraged by her familiarity with the name, I added that he was my uncle, or something like that. She assured me that I was quite mistaken. Embarrassed and on shaky ground, I let it go. But when I was in junior high school, I made a point of telling the music teacher that my grandmother had had a long affair with George Gershwin.

I was very adult, I thought, in my breezy reference to this celebrated or notorious or noteworthy happening or event or sequence of events. I can't recall the music teacher's name, but I can clearly remember the look of dismay on his face, his visible flinch at my casual deployment of the word "affair." He wasn't impressed—he was upset by my breeziness. We were both embarrassed and didn't speak of it again, though later in the term when the class studied a recording of the "Rhapsody in Blue" I felt him staring at me.

THE POSED STUDIO portraits of George in Ganz's apartment had dedications: "For Kay—Love—George" or "For Kay—Best—George," and some had a few musical bars sketched in along the bottom in his distinctive thick black penstrokes, his ink a singularly Gershwinesque black, the same emphatic ebony of his brilliantine hair and our Steinway piano. He was a sharp dresser, a little self-conscious, a little self-important. Famous-looking, somehow. By now I knew he had been dead a long while.

As I was born in 1955, there was a disappointing gulf of eighteen years between his death in 1937 and my birth. Most of the photographs had dates, and when I studied them I would always calculate anew how many years he had left to live at the time of each portrait. Three years. Two years.

But the photograph of George that fascinated me the most wasn't in my grandmother's apartment; it was in my mother's bedroom back in our house. It was actually a picture of my mother, a photograph taken and printed by George in 1932 (five years to live), when she was about ten. Now, some thirty-three years later, I was ten, and enjoying my close resemblance to her as a child. Some of my friends even believed me when I told them it was a picture of me. I wanted to be in that picture, to have been included in the excitement of being loved by the man who loved my mother's mother.

At ten, I study the photo continually. Seen in a mirror's reflection, George looms out of the shadows behind my staring mother, his Leica obscuring most of his face.

"Who's the creepy guy? Is that your dad?" one less than impressed school chum inquires. I am furious. Of course it's not my dad, who is rarely around and in any case isn't the least bit like George. I might not be capable of thinking about sexual attractiveness in adult terms at this point in my life, but George, in my books, is romantic, desirable, what a man ought to be like. Not anything like my own remote father, who never focuses on me in the way that George focuses on my mother.

The photograph *is* creepy when I look at it now. My mother's stare is disconcerting. Is she pensive, or terrified? My mother wears a black dress that's got a neckline far too mature for a child of ten. Has George dressed her for the picture? There's something a little bit like a Balthus painting in the pose, in the look. Has she been dressing up with her sisters? Is it possibly her mother's gown? Are they alone in this dim room lit only by candles? What, in any case, is he doing with his lover's middle child, taking those pictures of her, spending time with her in a darkroom, showing her how to develop and print?

And that wasn't just any darkroom. It was in the basement of Gregory Zilboorg's house. Dr. Zilboorg was a notorious psycho-analyst who counted among his analysands my grandmother, George, my grandfather, my grandfather's sister, my grandfather's second wife, my grandfather's cousin, and numerous other relations and friends. Incredibly, Dr. Zilboorg—"Gregory," as he was called in later years around my house (yet another mysterious quasi-relative to sort out)— had been a frequent houseguest under my grandparents' roof in those days.

It was Dr. Zilboorg who gave George his first camera and en-couraged his photography. George gave my mother her first camera for her tenth birthday. My mother and George were frequently alone together, working in Gregory's darkroom.

What of it? I am suspicious of my own suspicion. Is my con-temporary disapproval the dismay of a thoughtful parent of daugh-ters, or is it the jealous tattling of one who has been left out of the fun? Or is the real question about how my mother got from being the child in that photo, the object of George's gaze, to being the watcher, the woman of my childhood memories, a camera masking her face at every event?

WHEN MY GRANDMOTHER began her long affair with George Gersh-win in 1925, she was twenty-eight, the wife of a banker, the mother of three little girls. She was, I guess, a truly terrible mother. The life of many parties, she was mostly absent from the daily lives of her daughters.

When I interviewed the writer Madeleine L'Engle for a profile a few years ago, she happened to describe her first published piece of writing, a story originally written when she was a senior at Smith.

It concerns the very fancy household of a childhood friend, and it contains a vivid description of two little girls watching in silence while their very glamorous mother sits at her dressing table—her face glimpsed only in the mirror—getting ready to go out. For no particular reason, I asked the name of this childhood friend, and discovered that she was my aunt April, my mother's older sister. The woman in the mirror was, of course, my grandmother.

OF THE THREE daughters, only my mother, the middle one, remained close to her mother as an adult, both emotionally and geographically. Consequently, I had the opportunity from my earliest childhood to form my own relationship with Ganz, a gift from my mother for which I am profoundly grateful. While I may have been told too much, too soon, about Ganz, nothing was presented to me in especially judgmental terms. Otherwise, I might well have grown up as distant from my grandmother as some of my cousins, whose mothers, my two aunts, were a little angrier and less forgiving.

My mother's explanation to me for their attitudes was summarized thusly: they didn't like George. The story had the rhythms of a retold fairy tale as she would narrate, always in the same words, that the youngest sister was too young and only knew that George wasn't the same as Daddy; the oldest sister was too old and could see the threat, could see all too well what was going on and what was at risk; only the middle sister was just right, accepting, responsive, eager to please, happy for the attention. Only my mother had liked George, had enjoyed him, and he, in turn, had been enchanted by her. (*I* would have liked George, I would think to myself. He would have liked *me*, too.)

She taught him to tap-dance. He learned to ride on Denny, her horse, at the family's pre-Colonial country house in Greenwich where George lived and worked in the guest cottage for long periods of time when (the story goes) my grandfather was away on long business trips.

MY GRANDMOTHER WAS known to the world as Kay Swift. Born Katharine Faulkner Swift (I was named Katharine Swift for her), she was called Katharine by everyone including my grandfather, James Warburg, her first husband—and her first lyricist. It was George who started calling her Kay. They met at a party. (Not so coincidentally, the 1926 Gershwin show "Oh, Kay!" featured the posh Kay and Jimmy Winter.)

Kay and George were a glamorous couple when they were together at parties or the theater. They wafted through those years, flouting convention, having a good time, breaking all the rules. But no matter how much "fun" everyone was having, their romance caused tremendous pain for my grandfather and my mother and her sisters. (For years I have wondered if Kay and George were an inspiration for Thorne Smith—a frequent houseguest in Greenwich in those years—when he conjured up George and Marian, the ghostly madcap couple in his novel *Topper*, who blithely cause trouble but never have to pay the consequences.)

KATHARINE SWIFT BEGAN her musical life in the classical world. Her father was a distinguished music critic for a New York newspaper before his sudden death at age forty-five from appendicitis. Katharine worked to help support her mother and younger brother; my grandparents met because my grandmother was playing piano in a classical trio that had been hired to perform at the home of Adolph and Margaret Lewisohn, Warburg cousins.

But it seems likely that her attraction to popular music was connected to her attraction to George. It was George who persuaded Richard Rodgers to hire her as the rehearsal pianist for the 1927

Rodgers and Hart show, *A Connecticut Yankee*. Taking that job was a highly unusual move for the socialite wife of a banker, the mother of three young children.

My grandparents began to write Broadway show tunes together soon after that, and their first hit was "Can't We Be Friends?," which Libby Holman sang to Clifton Webb in *The First Little Show* in 1929. My grandfather didn't use the Warburg name, because it was thought that a banker who wrote show tunes might upset the investors, so for his pen name he reversed his first and middle names and became Paul James. If James Paul Warburg couldn't compete against George Gershwin for the affection of his own wife, maybe Paul James could.

Just as some couples have a baby in an attempt to save a marriage, it is my sense that my grandparents gave birth to a Broadway show. *Fine and Dandy* opened in 1930, halfway through my grandmother's decade-long affair with George. The title song is ubiquitous still.

One of the best songs in the score, a torchy number called "Nobody Breaks My Heart," contains my grandfather's wistful lyric: "Yes men, press men, lawyers and bankers/Don't give me that/for which my soul hankers/And no one, no one, nobody breaks my heart."

My grandparents divorced in 1935. George went to Hollywood soon after that and, it seems, his romance with my grandmother was put on hold. They both began to see other people, though my grandmother always said that they had an understanding that their relationship was unfinished business. George died of a brain tumor a year later, at thirty-eight. My grandmother once admitted to me that if he had lived she imagined that they might indeed have married, but probably also would have divorced.

Other people weren't so sure. Oscar Levant spotted them arriving at a nightclub and is said to have remarked, "Look—here comes George Gershwin with the future *Miss Kay Swift.*"

✻　　✻　　✻

FROM MY EARLIEST memories of her, Ganz was a lot of fun in a nerve-wracking sort of way. She misplaced theater tickets, or went on the wrong night. She overtipped wildly and walked so fast down the street it was hard to keep up with her. She was known to buy entire extravagant bunches of balloons from the vendors in Central Park decades before balloons were commonplace, inflatable greeting cards.

Perhaps because of her English mother, Ganz abbreviated in a Bertie Wooster–ish way, toasting at celebrations with several glasses of "champers," telling taxi drivers to go to "Mad Ave" or greeting friends on the phone with a habitual "How are things in gen?" Once, walking on the street with me, she spotted the open shirt of a hirsute construction worker and then asked if I agreed with her that "H.C." (hairy chests) were unattractive.

Though her picture was on the wall at Sardi's, she was famous only to the cognoscenti who had heard of her, and it pleased her immensely when she was asked for her autograph when she went to hear her friend Bobby Short, who sometimes sang her songs at the Cafe Carlyle.

Her 1943 book about her marriage to her second husband, a cowboy, was subsequently made into a movie, *Never a Dull Moment*, with Fred MacMurray as the cowboy and Irene Dunne as Kay. (When I was 18, my cousin Betsy and I spent a strange day with her second husband at a rodeo outside Spokane. John Wayne would have been better casting.) I must have seen that film a dozen times in my childhood, usually when I was home from school with a fever and the movie was shown on obscure television stations at odd times. I liked to imagine myself in the role of the cowboy's little girl, who was played by Natalie Wood.

Going out in public with Ganz when I was growing up felt like a high-wire balancing act of pride and embarrassment. I was a mortified twelve the night that Ganz, needing to attract a waiter in a restaurant, waved her napkin high in the air and called out, "Yoo hoo! Waiterkins!" (At a certain hour in the day, the perpetual cup of coffee was generally replaced by a perpetual "vod ton.") She once introduced me at a party to Ring Lardner, Jr., whose writing I admired, as "my friend Kathy," because she could not bring herself to admit that she had a granddaughter of sixteen.

Like most eccentrics, she was largely oblivious to her own eccentricities. Our only serious argument, ever, occurred when I was in my late teens, and it was on the subject of her wish to provide diction lessons for the unsophisticated fiancée of one of my cousins. I insisted that she refrain, that the offer would be offensive and insulting; Ganz ultimately conceded, wondering at the same time if the poor dear girl might not at least like to be treated to some electrolysis.

When I think about it now, it strikes me that my grandmother was astonishingly available to me as a child for someone so narcissistic and on stage all the time. I was, of course, a rapt audience. But she had a genuine warmth under all the showbiz hoopla. She knew the names of my stuffed animals. She loved to play Hearts or Casino or Gin on the floor, though she cried real tears over her Monopoly losses. (That, my mother explained to me, was because her hopelessness with money was all too real. After a certain point, we were actually forbidden to play Monopoly with Ganz.) She was a champion reader-out-loud.

Ganz gave off sparks of nervousness and excitement (manic tendencies, perhaps; too much coffee, for sure). From the time I was very little, she assumed that I too believed that life was filled with potential wonderfulness—an intriguing and sometimes confusing contrast to the chaotic and mostly depressed atmosphere in my own household. There, it seemed, the prevailing philosophy was that the past had been glorious and now the world was nobody's oyster. I felt very loved by her.

* \ * \ *

I LOVE MY husband for many reasons: his kindnesses, his passions, his intense devotion to our daughters Lucy and Charlotte, his sensibilities. But I don't doubt that the coffee in his shoes was truly an element in my early attraction. He smelled right. Why do we like the things we like? Psychoanalysts smile knowingly when we say something "just feels right" or is "the most natural thing."

My grandmother was still alive then, nearly eighty. Nick met her early on in our courtship—it seemed essential to me that they should know each other—because it was a way for each of them to know me, and because I knew that they would adore one another.

My mother's family was, in those days, still dominated by numerous elderly women whose preference for men over women was so pronounced that the term "male chauvinism" doesn't begin to describe it. They were themselves, of course, an exception to their beliefs that men were essentially superior. For them, the acquisition of a fine male specimen like Nick was probably my greatest accomplishment.

Nick understood this, and he also enjoyed basking in their approving glow from time to time. Nick was my gift to them, and they were my gift to Nick. Meanwhile, with the comfort and security of this alliance, instead of feeling perpetually like a steerage passenger attempting to mingle with my betters in first class, I could begin to laugh about the transparent hierarchies.

Nick's bond with my grandmother was instant and profound. He was no doubt caught up in my intense devotion to her, but, he says now, he was instantaneously moved by what he saw of her in me and of me in her. Our romance made my grandmother happy for me, but I think something about us as a couple also made Ganz happy in a vaguely narcissistic way, too. Though I am more unlike her than like her in my nature, I bear a certain physical resemblance to her, and am, after all, her namesake. Perhaps our alliance felt to all of us like an idealized redoing of the past, a better version, in which nobody dies and the couple gets to live happily ever after.

Nick and I spent quite a lot of time with her in our first months together. When we would go out to dinner, Ganz often asked that we provide her with an escort from among our friends. ("What if there's dancing?") When we told her we were getting married, Ganz was very excited and pleased—"And he has blue eyes! All of my husbands had blue eyes!" she blurted. (George, incidentally, had brown eyes.) We were married at my grandfather's house in Greenwich, owing to the generosity of my grandfather's widow, who certainly had no obligation to host our wedding. I was twenty and had no sense at all of what I was imposing by making that request.

Why did I want to be married there? It felt right. It was the most natural thing. The ceremony took place outside, in front of the millpond, in sight of the guest cottage where George had stayed. The music played right after the ceremony was an eccentric arrangement my grandmother had written for us, for flute and trombone, of "Love is Here to Stay," the last song George finished before he died. *Our love is here to stay* are the words inscribed inside our wedding rings.

When, a year later, we bought a ramshackle eighteenth-century house in Connecticut, Ganz speculated that we might consider building a guest cottage somewhere on the land. "A guest cottage can be very *convenient*," she told me.

WE'VE BEEN MARRIED now for twenty-one years and she's been dead for six years. When you've been married for a long time—this was something I didn't particularly anticipate—you become a repository, a private archive, of memories of your spouse's friends and relations as well as your own. Love is loving some or most of the people your partner loves, and then it is mourning and remembering them when they have died.

I love the way my husband loved my grandmother. He really had her number, too. Once, after spending the night in her guest room in order to get to an early meeting in the city, Nick sent her flowers with a card that read simply, "From the man who spent the night." Ganz was nearly ninety by then. She was so delighted with his flowers and card, her housekeeper revealed to me, that not only did she display them in the front hall for maximum exposure, but after they wilted, she replaced the flowers several times, each time putting the card back into the arrangement.

GROWING UP, I missed George Gershwin without ever knowing him, because two people I loved, my mother and my grandmother, loved him and missed him.

He doesn't haunt my dreams, but I often think about the way he changed my life. It is probable that the inheritance of wealth in my mother's family might have gone in different directions had my grandparents not divorced as they did. And my mother might have led a happier life, made a better marriage, if the territory of her own childhood had been less occupied by her mother's affair.

For the rest of her life, my grandmother dedicated much of her musical energy to preserving the Gershwin music that was still in her head. In her mid-eighties, she was still jotting down fragments of Gershwin pieces not known to the world, with careful notation about working titles and original keys. It occurs to me, as the administrator of her music copyrights today, that she could have simply claimed the Gershwin tunes known only to her as her own work and gone on to publish any number of successful hits, but she never did that.

If anything, the Gershwin music in her head obstructed and overwhelmed her own production. For a songwriter of her caliber, she wrote very little. A scholar working on a dissertation on Kay Swift has observed to me that there are enormous puzzling gaps in my grandmother's career, when she produced nothing; each of those gaps corresponds to periods when my grandmother was particularly active in her support of George's work. In his lifetime, this is so literally evident that there are bars of music in her handwriting on his manuscript pages. After his death, she spent years keeping the candle lit, traveling with productions of *Porgy and Bess,* consulting on various Gershwin revivals, and working with Ira Gershwin to complete a number of Gershwin songs based on extant fragments, some of which have more than a few bars of Kay Swift, though she always denied that publicly.

MY GRANDMOTHER'S AFFAIR with George Gershwin defined something for me about love and loss. I have never really understood how she came to make that dangerous leap, but her having done so was always an essential part of her, and a central aspect of my family's sensibility. Maybe the bittersweet consequence of her infidelity is why, after all these years, I am so committed to the vows of my own marriage. Looking back, I have often calculated at various points in my life what my grandmother's life was like when she was the same age. It is almost always unfathomable to contemplate what she was up to in contrast to what I have been up to. Her choices are appealing and might even seem inevitable when measured in terms of the glamour and excitement that used to dazzle me, but they remain unfathomable for being emotionally unsupportable. The heart wants what the heart wants, as that Gershwin connoisseur Woody Allen has observed. What's hard to take in after all these years is that my beloved grandmother's heart led her down such a destructive path.

Nick and I share a dependence on strong coffee every morning to begin our days. It's one of life's pleasures that we can't give up. The A&P coffee grinder has a special cabinet of its own in our kitchen. One weekend morning not so long ago, when we were lying in bed together with coffee and newspapers, the first few bars of "Love Is Here to Stay" came drifting up from the piano in the living room. Our younger daughter Charlotte had been working it out for a week, and now she had really got it. It was a moment that felt just right.

EXCERPTS FROM SWAN LAKE

PETER CAMERON

 WHAT IS THAT called again?" my grandmother asks, nodding at my lover's wok.

"A wok," I say.

"A wok," my grandmother repeats. The word sounds strange coming out of her mouth. I can't remember ever hearing her say a foreign word. She is sitting at the kitchen table smoking a Players cigarette. She saw an ad for them in *Time* magazine and wanted to try them, so after work I drove her down to the 7-Eleven and she bought a pack. She also bought a Hostess cherry pie. That was for me.

Neal, my lover, is stir-frying mushrooms in the wok. My grandmother thinks he is my friend. I am slicing tomatoes and apples. We are staying at my grandmother's house while my parents go on a cruise around the world. It is a romance cruise, stopping at the "love capitals" of the world. My mother won it. Neal and I are making mushroom curry. Neal isn't wearing a shirt, and his chest is sweating. He always sweats when he cooks. He cooks with a passion.

"I wish I could help," my grandmother says. "Let me know if I can."

"We will," says Neal.

"I don't think I've seen a wok before," my grandmother says.

"Everyone has them now," says Neal. "They're great."

The doorbell rings, the front door opens, and someone shouts, "Yoo-hoo!"

"Who's that?" I say.

"Who's what?" my grandmother says. She's a little deaf.

I walk into the living room to investigate. A woman in a jogging suit is standing in the front hall. "Who are you?" she says.

"Paul," I say.

"Where's Mrs. Andrews?" she asks.

"In the kitchen," I say. "I'm her grandson."

"Oh," she says. "I thought you were some kind of maniac. What with that knife and all." She nods at my hand. I am still holding the knife.

"Who are you?" I ask.

"Who's there?" my grandmother shouts from the kitchen.

The woman shouts her name to my grandmother. It sounds like Gloria Marsupial. Then she whispers to me, "I'm from Meals on Wheels. I bring Mrs. Andrews dinner on Tuesday nights. Your mother bowls on Tuesday."

"Oh," I say.

Mrs. Marsupial walks past me into the kitchen. I follow her. "There you are," she says to my grandmother. "I thought he had killed you."

"Nonsense," my grandmother says. "What are you doing here? You come on Tuesdays."

"It is Tuesday," says Mrs. Marsupial. She opens the oven. "We've got to warm this up."

"I don't need it tonight," my grandmother says. "They're making me dinner."

Mrs. Marsupial eyes the wok, the mushrooms, and Neal disdainfully.

"What do you have?" Neal asks.

Mrs. Marsupial takes a tinfoil tray out of the paper bag she is holding. It has a cardboard cover on it. "Meat loaf," she says. "And green beans. And a nice pudding."

"What kind of pudding?" my grandmother asks.

"Rice pudding," says Mrs. Marsupial.

"No thanks," says my grandmother.

"What are you making?" Mrs. Marsupial asks Neal.

"Mushroom curry," says Neal. "We're lacto-vegetarians."

"I'm sure you are," Mrs. Marsupial replies. She turns to my grandmother. "Well, do you want this or not?"

"I can have it tomorrow night," my grandmother says. "If I remember."

"Then I'll stick it in the fridge." Mrs. Marsupial opens the refrigerator and frowns at the beer Neal and I have installed. She moves a six-pack of Dos Equis aside to make room for the container. "I'll put it right here," she says into the refrigerator, "and tomorrow night you just pop it into the oven at about three hundred and warm it up, and it will be as good as new." She closes the refrigerator and looks at my grandmother. "Are you sure you're all right now?" she asks.

"What kind of bush is that out there?" my grandmother says. She points out the window.

"That's not a bush, dear," Mrs. Marsupial says. "That's the clothesline."

"I know that's the clothesline," my grandmother says. "I mean behind it. With the white flowers."

"It's a lilac bush," I say.

"A lilac? Are you sure?"

"It's a lilac," confirms Neal. "You can smell it when you hang out the wash." He opens the window and sticks his head out. "You can smell it from here," he says. "It's beautiful."

"Do you want me to take your blood pressure?" Mrs. Marsupial asks my grandmother. "I left the sphygmomanometer in the van."

"No," my grandmother says. "My blood pressure is fine. It's my memory that's no good."

I dump the sliced tomatoes and apples into the wok and lower the domelike cover. Then I stick my head out the window beside Neal's. It's getting dark. The lilac bush, the clothesline, the collapsing grape arbor are all disappearing.

"I don't want to be late for my next drop-off," Mrs. Marsupial says. "I guess I'll be running along."

No one says anything. Neal has taken my hand; we are holding hands outside the kitchen window where my grandmother and Mrs. Marsupial can't see us. The smell of curry mixes with the scent of lilacs and intoxicates me. I feel as if I'm leaning on the balcony of a Mediterranean villa, not the window of my grandmother's house in Cheshire, Connecticut, five feet above the dripping spigot.

AFTER DINNER MY grandmother tells Neal and me stories about "growing up on the farm." She didn't really grow up on a farm— she just visited a friend's farm one summer—but these memories are particularly vivid and make for good telling. I have heard them many times, but Neal hasn't. He is lying on the floor at my feet, exhausted from cooking. My grandmother is sitting on the love seat and I am sitting across from her on the couch, stroking Neal's bare back with my bare foot, a gesture that is hidden by the coffee table. At least I think it is.

"There was an outhouse with a long bench and three holes—a little one, a medium one, and a big one."

"Like the three bears," says Neal. His eyes are closed.

"Like who?" says my grandmother. She doesn't like being interrupted.

"The three bears," repeats Neal. "Cinderella and the three bears."

"Goldilocks," I correct.

"Little Red Riding Hood," murmurs Neal.

"You've lost me," my grandmother says. "Anyway, we used to eat outside, on a big plank table under a big tree. Was it an oak tree? No, it was a mulberry tree. I remember because mulberries would fall off it if the wind blew. You'd be eating mashed potatoes and suddenly there would be a mulberry in them. They looked like black raspberries. In between courses we would run down to the barn and back—down the hill to the barn, touch it, and run back up the hill. You'd always be hungry again when you got back up." She pauses. "We should turn on some light," she says. "We shouldn't sit in the dark."

No one says anything. No one turns on a light, because light damages the way that words travel. Suddenly my grandmother says, "How many times was I married?"

"Once," I say. "Just once."

"Are you sure just once?"

"As far as I know."

"Maybe you had affairs," suggests Neal.

"Oh, I'm sure I had affairs," says my grandmother. "Although I couldn't tell you with whom. I can't remember the faces at all. It all gets fuzzy. Sometimes I'm not even sure who you are."

"I'm Paul," I say. "Your beloved grandson."

"I'm Neal," Neal says. "Paul's friend."

"I know," my grandmother says. "I know now. But I'll wake up tonight and I'll have no idea. I won't even know where I am. Or what year it is."

"But none of that matters," I say.

"What?" my grandmother asks.

"Who cares what year it is?" I say. I rest both my feet lightly on Neal's back. It moves as though he is sleeping. I think about explaining how none of that matters: names or ages or whereabouts. But, before I can explain this to my grandmother, or attempt to, a new thought occurs to me: Someday, I'll forget Neal, just like my grandmother has forgotten the great love of her life. And then I think: Is Neal the great love of my life? Or is that one still coming, to be forgotten, too?

AFTER MY GRANDMOTHER goes to bed at nine o'clock, Neal and I redo the dishes. She likes to wash them if we make the dinner, but she doesn't do such a hot job anymore. There are always little pieces of muck stuck to her pink glass plates. Neal washes and I dry. I am using a dishtowel from the 1964 World's Fair. On it, a geisha girl embraces an Eskimo, who in turn embraces an Indian squaw embracing a man in a kilt. My grandmother took my sister and me to the World's Fair, but I don't remember her buying this dishtowel.

"I think I'm going to move back into the apartment," Neal says.

"Why?" I ask.

"I feel funny here. I don't feel comfortable."

"But I thought you wanted to get out of the city in the summer?"

"I did. I do. But this isn't working out." Neal motions with his wet, sudsy hand, indicating my grandmother's kitchen: the African violets on the windowsill, the humming refrigerator, the cookie jars filled with Social Teas. I insert the plate I am drying into the slotted dish rack. It seems to stand on its own accord, gleaming.

"Are you mad?" asks Neal.

"I don't know," I say. "Sad. But not mad."

"There is another thing, too," Neal says. He chases the suds down the drain with the sprayer thing.

"What?"

"I feel like when we're sleeping together she might come in. I don't feel right about it."

"She sleeps all night," I say. "She thinks you sleep on the porch. Plus she's senile."

"I know," says Neal, "but I still don't feel right about it. I just can't relax."

I sit down at the kitchen table and light one of my grandmother's Players cigarettes. Neal washes his hands, dries them, and carefully folds the World's Fair dishtowel. He comes over and curls his fingers around my throat, lightly, affectionately throttling me. Neal's clean hands smell like the English Lavender soap my grandmother keeps in a pump dispenser by the sink. Neal's hands smell like my grandmother's hands.

I exhale and look at our reflection in the window. I only smoke about one cigarette a month, and every time I do I experience a wonderful dizzy feeling that quickly gives way to nausea.

"It's no big deal," Neal says. "It's just not cool here."

I think about answering, but I can't. I close my eyes and feel myself floating. The occasional cigarette is a wonderful thing.

MY MOTHER SENDS me a postcard from Piraeus. This is what it says:

> Dear Paul,
> Piraeus is a lovely city considering I had never even heard of it. I'm not sure why it's a Love Capital except the movie "Never on Sunday" was filmed here. Have you seen it? Hope you're O.K. Are you taking good care of Grandma?
>
> Love,
> Mom

About a week after Neal moves out, the ballet comes to town, and my grandmother asks to see it. There are commercials for it on TV, showing an excerpt from *Swan Lake*, while across the bottom of the screen a phone number for charging tickets appears and disappears. The swan's feet blur into the flashing numbers.

My grandmother claims she has never been to the ballet. I don't know if I should believe her or not. Whenever the commercial comes on, she turns it up loud and calls for me to come watch. I do not understand her sudden zeal for the ballet. She gave up on movies long ago, because they were "just nonsense." Besides, she falls asleep at nine o'clock, no matter where she is.

Nevertheless, I buy three tickets to *Swan Lake* for my grandmother's eighty-eighth birthday. Neal comes to her special birthday dinner, bringing a Carvel ice-cream cake with him. At my grandmother's request, we are eating tomatoes stuffed with tuna salad. She must have seen an ad for it somewhere. I tried to scallop the edges of the tomatoes as she described, but I failed: they looked hacked-at, like something that would be served in a punk restaurant. But they taste O.K.

"It's just like old times, having Neal here," my grandmother says.

"I've only been gone a week," Neal says.

"It seems like longer," my grandmother says. "It seems like ages. We were lonely without you. Weren't we, Paul?"

I don't answer. I never admit to being lonely.

After dinner Neal and I do the dishes because my grandmother is the birthday girl and not allowed to help. Neal is telling her the story of *Swan Lake*. "The chief swan turns into a girl and falls in love with the prince, but then she gets turned back into a swan."

"Why?" my grandmother asks.

"I don't know," Neal says. "It's morning or something. They have to part. But the prince goes back to the lake the next night and finds her, and because they truly love one another, she changes back into a girl. I think that's it. Basically."

"It sounds ridiculous," says my grandmother.

"I thought you especially wanted to see *Swan Lake*," I say.

"I do," my grandmother says. "It just sounds silly." She looks out the window. "What kind of bush is that out there?" She points to the lilac bush.

"A lilac," I say.

"That's a lilac?" she says. "I thought lilacs had tiny purple flowers."

"They do," I say. "But that's a white lilac. The flowers grow in bunches."

"That's not a lilac," my grandmother says. "I remember lilacs."

"It is a lilac," says Neal. "Maybe you're thinking of wisteria. Or dogwood."

"I can't see it from here," my grandmother says. "I'm going to go out and look at it." She gets up and walks down the hall. The back door opens and then slams shut.

"If she asks me that one more time," I say, "I think I'll go crazy."

"I think it's sweet," Neal says. "I think your grandmother's great."

"I know," I say. "She is."

Neal puts the remaining, melting Carvel cake back into the freezer, and then stands there, with the freezer door open, pinching the pink sugar roses with his fingers. "I wish your grandmother knew we were lovers," he says.

I laugh. "I don't think she'd want to know that," I say. I sit down at the kitchen table.

"Why do you say that?" Neal says. "I think you should tell her. I wouldn't be surprised if she had figured it out."

"What do you mean?" I say.

"What do you mean, what do I mean?" Neal says.

"She doesn't know," I say. "No one knows."

"I know no one knows." Neal closes the freezer and sits down next to me. "That's the problem."

I look out the window. My grandmother is walking slowly down the backyard. She is an old lady, and I love her, and I love Neal, too, but I don't see the problem in all this. "I don't see the problem in all this," I say.

"You don't?" Neal says. "Really, you don't?"

I shake my head no. Neal shrugs and gets up. He opens the refrigerator and stands silhouetted in the glow from the open door. He is looking for nothing in particular. Outside, my grandmother reaches up and pulls a lilac blossom toward her face, because she has forgotten what they are.

NEAL IS DISGUSTED with me, and leaves the ballet at intermission. My grandmother falls asleep as Prince Siegfried is reunited with Odette. Her hands are crossed in her lap. She is wearing a pair of white mismatched gloves—one has tiny pearls sewn on the back of the hand, and the other doesn't.

I watch the dancing, unamused. The ballet is such a lie. No one—not my grandmother, not Neal, not I—no one in real life ever moves that beautifully.

LOVE IN THE LAND OF LOSS

CAROLINE LEAVITT

I WAS MARRIED in a state of terror. I stood frozen under the *chupah* in an Italian restaurant in New York City, surrounded by a small, exuberant coterie of friends and family, and at the rabbi's very first words, I began to sob so uncontrollably I was hysterical. My husband-to-be took my hand and held it tight, but I wept through my wedding ceremony, crying so hard that my mascara streamed down my cheeks and my nose ran. Out of the corner of my eye I spotted outstretched hands offering Irish linen handkerchiefs and pastel tissues which I blindly grabbed and pressed to my face. I wept because I knew I was tempting disaster. I wept because I knew I was playing it unsafe. I wept because I was thirty-eight years old and waiting for my history to repeat itself, and for the man I now loved more than life itself to suddenly and inexplicably die just moments before we would be man and wife.

MY DISTRESS WAS not so crazy since every future is seeded in a past. In 1987, two weeks before another wedding, back when I believed that the universe had sense and order, that happiness was a reward for good behavior, and that love could last forever, my fiancé died and took my life and my logical thinking along with him. He suffered a heart attack so massive that not even a miracle could have saved him.

There's no preparation for this kind of shock, no making peace, no coming to terms. Instead, ground gives way. The earth quakes. And however you can, you run for cover. I spent nearly two years roaming the country, traveling away from my grief and talking to whomever might give me back any sort of future: priests who told me to trust God's plan, rabbis who told me there *was* no plan, turbaned psychics who took one look at my red-rimmed eyes and told me this was going to be my happiest year yet. When my money ran out, I returned to New York. I began to think that the only expert help I might find was from other people like myself, and so I joined a Young Widows' Group.

My group met every Thursday at a small hall, right before the Alcoholics Anonymous people. There were ten women, age eighteen to forty, all of whom acted as if they had known me forever. They sat beside me on the plush couches and made me fragrant herbal tea. They rubbed what tension they could from my shoulders and stroked my hair. And then, to my absolute horror, they told me with great assurance: "You will never have love like you had before. You will always be damaged." One woman smiled meaningfully at me. "But," she emphasized, "you will always have us."

I lasted a month in this group. I kept going because it filled up the hours, and in the end, the group did turn out to be a kind of salvation, though not in the way I would have expected. Since this was a club that I didn't want membership in, I began to react against it with defiance. When they told me my friends would abandon me in my grief, I brought colleagues and neighbors to the meetings to prove them wrong. When they told me I would need to come to the group for years, if not for a lifetime, I gathered my things and announced, "I quit." Then I ran down the stairs, their voices calling after me, tightening like a lasso.

But even out of the group, I carried those young widows with me. I kept hearing their voices, a Greek chorus of despair. "If you loved your fiancé, you won't want a new love anyway," they chanted, "because, well—death doesn't end a relationship and new love is a betrayal." And so, a few months later, desperate to prove them wrong, I grappled with my sorrow and began to date.

Nothing took. I saw a man who was in love with the idea of young widowhood because it seemed so romantic. "The scarred are more interesting, don't you think?" he kept asking. "They have such *depth*." But I knew how easily you could drown in the depths, and I left him. I spent a few weeks with a man who kept trying to compete with my dead fiancé, who wanted to know what foods he had relished, what books he had loved, what movies he had cherished. Then I spent a year with a man with whom I had nothing in common, a man I had nevertheless agreed to marry only because I knew if I didn't, he would leave me, and then I would be alone with my misery.

He left anyway. "You have no ability to love," he informed me coolly, and I suspected that he might be right. I went into private grief counseling, and six months later a friend insisted I meet someone she swore I'd like. "I doubt it," I said.

His name was Jeff. He was thirty-eight, an editor and writer, smart and funny and handsome, a movie and book-aholic like me, and an unabashed romantic. And my friend was right. I did like him, so hard and so fast that I was torn between the relief at having something else to think about and the fear that if I got too cozy, the relationship might be taken from me instantly. To risk loving again meant to risk loss—and loss the second time around seemed more than any heart, no matter how elastic, could bear.

"So," I said casually, on one of our first dates. "Any incidence of heart problems in your family? Your father still alive? Your uncles?" Amused, patient, and knowing something about my past, he not only answered, he offered to show me his bill of health, "so clean, it squeaks," he said. I gave him the third degree about his health almost every time I saw him. If I could have tucked a blood pressure monitor and a stethoscope into my purse, I would have. Instead, I watched surreptitiously what Jeff ate and how he exercised. When I took his hand, I sometimes tried to time his pulse, and the funny thing was, that even after finding out that he was healthy, it didn't calm me. Instead, it made me more anxious, because to my utter astonishment, I was falling in love.

TWO YEARS INTO our relationship, we were in Venice, the most romantic place I had ever been. It was a cold and damp November. Jeff and I were gliding on a gondola at night, moving through a darkness pronged with stars. "Marry me," Jeff blurted and I bolted away from him. "You don't love me?" he asked, stunned.

I loved him more than anyone or anything, but I knew all too well what marriage meant. Say yes and then get ready to say goodbye. We got off the gondola and went to sit in a rain-soaked plaza, talking for two hours, miserable and tense, both convinced we were about to lose the other. "Maybe if we just live together," I tried to convince him. "Maybe if we just take it really, really slow." We gripped each other. We held on fast. "All right," he said finally. "When you're ready, you propose to me."

I DON'T KNOW what made me ready. Maybe it was another year of increasing happiness. And maybe, it was a memory of all those young widows, stubborn and stuck in their pasts. I could be different. I could have faith that perhaps this time, love might last, if only I were brave enough to chance it. "Think about what you really want," someone in the widows' group had said acidly in one meeting, "and then go out and try to get it. You want love in your life? Just see how far you get. Just see how life slams you." *It doesn't have to mean you*, I told myself. *Don't listen to that. Don't hear.*

I knew what I wanted: a husband, a home, a baby. I thought I had lost everything once when my fiancé died, but I had found it again—and myself—by risking loving Jeff. Why shouldn't I have a home and a baby, too? What do you have to lose, I kept asking myself, but I knew the answer hammering away inside of me: *everything.*

AND SO WE married, planning everything quickly, a ruse designed to trick my terror into subsiding. And throughout the ceremony, I sobbed so loudly that the rabbi's voice rose and fell like waves to accommodate my noise. And then, with streaky face and pink nose, the bodice of my velvet dress damp from my tears, I stepped back to examine my new husband in wonder. He was alive, breathing, smiling triumphantly at me. "Surprise," he said.

I TRIED TO relax. I knew Jeff was healthy. He went for checkups; he didn't smoke or drink and he was a vegetarian. But I was still a product of my past, and I woke up nights to watch his chest rise and fall with each breath. When he was ten minutes late to meet me, I panicked.

Loss can make you doubt happiness. Happiness can make you expect loss. I kept waiting for the other shoe to drop.

"There is no other shoe," Jeff insisted.

Ah, but then I became pregnant.

I CONVINCED MYSELF that I had more than paid my dues; my proof was that fate had rewarded me for my struggle with a marriage so happy that it never failed to astonish me. But when you turn a corner, you can still look around and feel where you've been. The old dirty, dark, and dangerous neighborhood hasn't disappeared. Thugs can still come out and grab you. Gunfire can still fell you from blocks away. Move on, I kept telling myself. Move on. You never know how things are going to turn out, and a life can be changed in an instant by a miracle as easily and inexplicably as it can by a tragedy.

Life was full of surprises. I was actually going to form my own *family*. I might not exactly be the optimum age for giving birth, but I was healthy and strong, and under the care of the top high risk obstetrician in New York. High risk. Absolutely. It was my middle name.

My doctor's waiting room was usually so full of worry, it was palpable, but I strode in, sometimes the only beaming woman there. Other women might complain about their roster of symptoms, but I had a new positive attitude. Everything began to delight me: the neverending morning sickness that crept well into evening, the surprising tight-wired cramps, the sleepless nights, the backaches. Even the thought of labor was a new and wonderful opportunity I couldn't wait to experience. "Get the net," a friend said, listening to me.

Don't get me wrong. High risk was one thing, insurance was another. I took extra care. I had every prenatal test imaginable: sonograms, amniocentesis, scans and measures. I called my doctor at the slightest twinge. I not only read every baby book I could get my hands on, I memorized entire chapters. I ate well and exercised and even managed to meditate, visualizing a baby so beautiful it seemed to shine. And I bonded with the baby, walking around with my hand over my belly, comforting and massaging and showering with love what was little more than a speed bump of a boy. I carried his sonogram picture in my wallet like a prized snapshot and took it out of its plastic liner so many times to show it off, to admire it myself, that it soon grew tattered. When my son grew big enough to be able to detect sound from the womb, I began to speak to him constantly, and to sing the Beatles' "I Will," chosen because I loved the affirmation. "I will, I will, I will," I kept repeating. I told myself it was a song he might recognize when he was born; it might remind him of how deeply I had loved and cared for him even as he swam in my womb.

JEFF AND I commemorated every step of my pregnancy. We called the baby by name—Max—to give him presence. We videotaped our baby as he moved inside my belly, pushing limbs out, making himself known. We stood in the center of his nursery with as much amazement as kids who have discovered that everyone was wrong, that Santa Claus *is* real, that he has read our wish lists and he's got our presents with him.

The entire time I was pregnant, I felt so healthy and happy and blessed that I began to tell myself, like a mantra I might believe in: *Everything is all right.*

MAX WAS A routine C-section. I lay with my arms strapped to a table, waiting, anxious, dazed and woozy from the anesthesia. Beside me, dressed in green surgical scrubs, Jeff held my hand. When he burst into tears, I felt a clip of fear. "Something's wrong," I thought. I knew what it was. The other shoe. A high-heeled stiletto. A steel-toed boot. And then I looked up, over the green scrub curtain, and there was our son, held up, coated with vernix and blood. He was like moonlight. His eyes were wide open and when they met mine, a constellation opened up inside of me. I fell in love. And then I shut my eyes and my whole life changed.

THIS IS WHAT I remember. Floating. Waking up in a hospital bed with a strange doctor hovering over me. "Do you know where you are?" he said. "Do you know what's happened to you?" I blinked, trying to focus. "Who are you?" I said.

On the window of the room was a taped picture of Max, lying on his side in the nursery bassinet, one hand outstretched, reaching towards me. GET WELL SOON MOMMY, I MISS YOU, LOVE MAX, it said. He misses me, I thought. But where had I been? And where was he?

"What's happened?"

"You've been comatose for two weeks."

Two weeks. What had happened two weeks ago to derail my life? And where was my family?

"We nearly lost you," the doctor said. I watched his mouth moving, forming words. "You've been very sick. You have a Factor Eight Inhibitor," he said.

Inhibitor. I heard the word. Inhibit. To slow. To stop.

"Where's my son?" I said.

But the doctor kept talking, telling me about a blood condition I had that kept my blood from clotting. It was, he said, an illness so rare it took a world-famous hematologist at the hospital to identify it and four operations to stop my bleeding. "We think we can treat it. And we know that in postpartum women, it goes away. We think you're going to be just fine."

"Where's Max?" I asked. "Where's Jeff?"

"Your whole family was here," the doctor said. "From Boston. From Maryland. Your friends. Every day."

"Where?" I whispered. "When?" I tried to pull myself up and the room narrowed into white.

I WAS A traveler again in the Land of Loss, only this time the borderlines were skewed, the maps I had relied on before were unreadable and crumpled, and I didn't know the language. My husband was missing. My baby. And two weeks of my own life.

"You're a very lucky woman," the nurses kept saying. "Look how well you're doing now."

"Where's my family?" I kept asking.

"Your husband will be here this evening," a nurse assured me. I glanced at her name tag. Cindy, it said. And then I fell asleep, drugged, exhausted, and when I woke, there was another woman I didn't know, stroking my hand lovingly, gazing at me with a kind of reverence. "I was in the delivery room with you," she told me. "I prayed and prayed to God for your recovery." I blinked at her. I tried to ask her, had she seen Jeff? Had she seen my baby? I was sure a woman who prayed to God for a stranger wouldn't lie. "Wait—" I tried to make my mouth move, but a current of exhaustion pulled me back to sleep.

When I woke later, there were three new doctors standing around my bed, discussing my case. When they saw me struggling to sit up, they smiled. "Welcome back," they said.

"Where's my husband and my baby?"

"Your husband was here this morning."

"No," I insisted. "He wasn't."

"You don't remember, that's all. He was here for three hours. I spoke with him myself."

I shook my head again. "Seeing is believing," I said.

One of the doctors half-smiled. "Not when you're on morphine," he said. "You've got to give yourself some time."

TIME STRETCHED LIKE elastic. For weeks, I hallucinated on morphine. I cried for the baby. I cried for Jeff. Doctors with cement blocks for heads came in and out of the room. For two nights I was convinced the hospital had moved me to a doctor's sex retreat where I was trapped, listening to seduction scenes played against the garbled strains of Isaac Hayes. Next to me was a woman in a blue-and-white dotted Swiss party dress and blue patent-leather T-strapped shoes. She was tied to a wheelchair, with a combination safe over her head. Her right foot tapped out the beat of the music. Panicked, I spotted Cindy the nurse and grabbed for her.

"Call my husband," I begged.

"Why, honey, he was just here."

"No, he wasn't."

"Why sugar, he visits you every day."

I began to rant. Cindy was lying to me. The hospital was lying to me. "Where's my husband? Where's my baby? What happened to them?" I kept asking. "What did you do with them?" I fell back onto the bed, suddenly cold with terror. "Are they dead?" I asked.

"Honey," Cindy soothed, stroking my hand. "They're as alive as you are. It's just the medication making you think such things." She studied me for a moment. "Why would we let you keep a picture of that gorgeous baby on your window if he was dead? Wouldn't that be sadistic? Your husband and your baby are alive. Just keep telling yourself that because it's the truth."

They're alive, I thought. Alive. It's the truth.

A week passed. And then another. And then I was waking from a dream, rousing myself from sleep. Someone was holding my hand. Another stranger, I thought. Another person saying welcome back, or another person pricking my veins, siphoning blood or transfusing it, measuring all the vital signs except the ones that make us the most vital: emotion. The hand on mine lightly tapped. I opened my eyes.

Jeff's face swam into focus. He was beside me. He was smiling. I burst into tears.

"You're alive," I said in wonder. I reached out to touch him, to make him real, and then I couldn't let go. "You're alive. That's incredible."

"So are you. That's more incredible."

"Is Max alive?'

He kissed my fingers. "Of course he is. He's beautiful."

"Where is he?"

"It's too infectious in here. He's got to get a little older before he can visit. He's at home with the baby nurse."

"He's really alive? He's really okay?"

Jeff bent and kissed my hair. "He's as okay as I am. As okay as you're going to be."

"Honest? This is the truth?"

Jeff smiled. "I can prove it to you."

"Prove it now."

Jeff smiled again. "All good things come to those who wait," he ordered. "You're just going to have to trust me on this one."

He stayed two hours past visiting hours, but not one of the nurses even lifted an eyebrow at him to leave. The nurses glided by, ushering other visitors out, reminding parents and friends that patients needed their sleep, but when they passed by us, they simply smiled or nodded.

"Looking good," one nurse said. "The both of you."

As she rushed by, her hands filled with clean linens, Cindy winked. "Now, didn't I tell you?" she said to me.

Jeff stayed until I had slept a little, and was calm enough to believe that he was alive and well, that he'd be back tomorrow, and the next day, and the next.

"I'll call you as soon as I get home," he said, "I have a surprise for you, anyway."

"What surprise?"

"Uh uh. You have to wait."

I couldn't sleep after he left. At first, I kept replaying his visit, making it indelible in my mind. He's alive, he's alive, he's alive, I kept repeating to myself. Then I began wondering about the surprise he had talked about. And then, as the hospital began to quiet down for the night, I began to imagine disaster. Car accidents. Burglars. Random Acts of God. I sat up, panicking, and then the phone rang.

"I told you I'd call," Jeff said. His voice was a tide, pulling me back to shore.

"I feel better," I lied.

"Well, you'll feel even more spectacular in a second," Jeff assured me. "You hang on. Someone wants to talk to you."

"Who?" I asked, thinking it was another friend who might have flown in, or a neighbor, or maybe the baby nurse, and suddenly there was babbling, soft and high-pitched. "Say hi to your son," Jeff said.

I bolted up in bed so fast it made me dizzy. I held the receiver so close to my ear it left marks. And then I began to talk to my son, telling him how sorry I was to have missed his first six weeks, how I would make it up to him, reminding him of how I had massaged him through my belly, how I had sung to him. "Max," I said. "It's Mommy." I said his name over and over, linked with mine, like a mantra which might bless us both.

THE NEXT DAY, Jeff began to bring in photos of Max. Fifteen color shots of my son sleeping, playing, in the car seat, on the sofa. I held each shot up ten times a day and had him tape them on the window, and by my bed, so no matter where I looked, I'd see Max.

The next week, Jeff brought in a home movie. The nurses wheeled us into their training room and I watched my son in his first bath, in his stroller, babbling and carrying on and fussing. When the video was over I sat up. "Play it again," I insisted. We were in the training room for almost three hours, and that night was the first time since I had been in the hospital that I slept through the night, deep and dreamless, and as absolutely content as it was possible for me to be.

If I don't remember the two weeks I had lost, the memories of the following weeks are indelible. The more Jeff visited, the more photos and tapes and phone calls he inundated me with, the better I began to feel. "Blood count's up," the doctors told me. "We're all really pleased."

"So can I go home?" I asked.

"Well, no—" the doctor admitted.

"So what can I do?"

"Well," said the doctor, breaking into a grin. "You're well enough now so that Max can come to visit you."

I WAS AS anxious as if I were going on a blind date. I made Jeff go out and buy cosmetics: eyeliner, eyeshadow, mascara, and lipstick. I wrote down the shades I wanted, the brands I preferred. I wanted a new hairbrush and tiny gold hoop earrings since I was convinced they were good luck. "Will he know me?" I kept asking, but what I was thinking was: Will he like me?

The night before Max's visit, I awoke at five in the morning. I gathered up my supplies and hobbled to the bathroom. My hands were still shaking. My legs buckled. I couldn't stand without leaning against the sink. I washed myself and changed into a new hospital gown, reattaching the IVs like an expert. Then I applied my makeup, trying not to smear the mascara, not to get the lipstick on my teeth. I brushed my long hair. When I got back into bed it was only 5:15. Five more hours. When the first round of doctors came, they blinked at me. "You look good," one doctor decided. "Your color's better."

"Thank Maybelline," I said.

At nine in the morning, I was wheeled into the solarium. A couple sat in the corner, whispering, sharing a cheese sandwich. Jeff and the baby nurse, a woman I recognized from the video and the photographs, were beaming at me, and in Jeff's arms was Max, dressed in a bright red outfit.

"I'd know you anywhere," I said, and Max was put in my arms. He stared, straining against me, turning and reaching for the baby nurse, reaching for Jeff. "Look at Mommy," Jeff coaxed, pivoting the baby towards me. Max began to cry. The couple gave me an annoyed look, and Max began to wail, his voice tight as a wire in the silence, rising up to another decibel.

"He's tired—" the nurse said, apologetically, reaching for him, but I kept my arms wound tightly around my son. And then I did the only thing I could think to do. I began to sing. "I Will." Our bonding song.

Max quieted. "Look," Jeff said in a hushed voice. "Look at that." There was no sound in the room except for my out-of-tune raspy voice. There was no motion except for my arms, rocking my own, my baby, my son.

TWO WEEKS LATER, I come home to my family. *Family.* I keep saying that word over and over, savoring it. I'm part of a family! We all troop to the doctors three times a week for my blood tests, my blood work, the surgeon's report. "You'll be completely cured," everyone says. "It's a miracle. And just a matter of time." *I could have this,* I think. *It could be all right.* Every morning, before Max wakes and wants his bottle, before Jeff rouses to fetch it for him and bring them both to me, I stand in front of the mirror staring at my ruined body, a map of stitches, bandaged in gauze. I look at myself, how changed I am, inside and out. And then Jeff comes in with the baby and settles Max, a sweetly intoxicating presence, against my shoulder. And then Jeff kisses my face, and then my stomach. "You are beautiful," he says. "And I am insane with love."

They say that after a forest fire, the destroyed trees make the soil richer and more capable of nurturing growth than ever before. You could take it as a metaphor for life, because as the capacity for pain grows, so does the capacity for joy. And when you know that sadness can visit at any time, your appreciation for happiness is over-powering.

I think again of the young widows who were in my group. They were beautiful women who had been attending the meetings for years, and I don't blame them now for their self-imposed insulation. Now

I understand how staying put might feel safer, how to love again might seem the most dangerous act of all.

"You've had a rough time of it," some people tell me. But I don't see it that way. Because at forty-four I have a baby and a husband. I'm alive and healthy. I'm loved. *I get to have this,* I keep telling myself in wonder. And then what I feel most is blessed.

MY BELT

LARRY O'CONNOR

SINCE I CAN remember, I'd been saving Paris. After college, when all my friends were traveling to Europe, I stayed home. I wanted to be ready. I wanted to go with the woman I loved, strolling the Champs-Élysées, buying postcards along the Seine, listening to street musicians playing for a sou. Over the years, romances bloomed, then faded, and when I did get married, our working lives and a baby got in the way. Finally, after eight years without a honeymoon, I convinced M. that it was time to go.

The night before the day we were to leave, I climbed the stairs with drinks and surprised M., who was sitting in bed propped up with pillows reading a novel. I looked at M. over my glass of an expensive French wine—white and chilled the way she liked it—and she returned the gaze over her reading glasses. "In Paris," I said as she pushed her glasses to the top of her head, "in Paris, you'll see, everything will be all right." We would sleep late, stop worrying about the bills piling up, the leaks from the roof that were staining the bedroom walls. We'd walk the streets of Hugo, savor the paintings by Degas, the sculptures of Rodin. *Un autre espresso? Croissant? Un morceau de pain? Certainement. Pourquoi pas?*

M. put down her book on the bedside table. "Some wine?" I offered. "But of course," she replied. She tossed an overstuffed pillow aside and inched closer to me as I poured from the bottle. "Imagine foie gras like you've never tasted, desserts made in heaven," she said. "Did you know that even in the best restaurants people bring their dogs? There's a place in the Bois du Boulogne where a couple bring a Great Pyrenees. It lies on the floor, perfectly behaved, before a roaring fire." She sipped slowly. "Waiters weave in and out around the dog like magic. Never miss a beat."

M. put down her wine and we kissed. We hadn't kissed like that in ages. In recent months, M. and I had taken to reading novels or looking at mediocre videos before bed, dropping off to sleep with just a peck on the lips. Now she was wide awake. I took a long, delicious drink, then started sneezing. Sulfites. We'd gotten a cat a few months before and I'd developed an allergy and wine with sulfites only made it worse. Hacking and wheezing, I ran past M. into the bathroom, pressed the atomizer into my mouth, and squeezed.

The next day we were an hour early at Newark International Airport. M. was in the ladies' room when I noticed a young woman in a wheelchair and her handsome companion exchange lovers' smiles. He reached for her hand and she arched her back. With her free hand, she grabbed the nape of his neck and pulled him close. The woman wore a plunging blue top and the man nestled his head in the V of her breasts, first brushing her skin lightly with his lips, then laying his head gently on her like silk.

Finally, M. returned, her eyelashes curled, cheeks rouged for the Newark-to-Paris night flight. I drew M. to me and hugged her. "What is it?" she whispered, sensing the change in me.

"In Paris," I said, "everything will be all right."

She smiled, tweaked my nose. "In Paris, they discovered sulfites."

I kissed her and raised the tickets before us like a torch as we approached airport security. Before putting down our carry-on I noticed the lover was now sitting in the wheelchair. The woman was nowhere to be seen.

LIKE MOST PEOPLE, expectations make me anxious. The larger the expectation the more nervous I become. When it comes to romance I've always been in conflict. Bring flowers, light candles, establish the mood. Then poof! Nothing. It's too forced, not natural. A woman expects the particulars of romance, yet in my experience love vanishes under the pressure of such attention.

Spontaneity wasn't my thing, either. Only fools rush in, I was told as a boy. I've always been someone who saves the best for last. I was the child who separated my Halloween candy, hoarding my favorites, the caramels and peanut butter cups. I'd leave them for so long that they'd get so stale I couldn't eat them. If only, I'd wish at times, I were an insatiable taker, someone who feasted on the best, the ripest, and then, when appetite waned, left the rest; a man who loved and lost, loved and lost, married, divorced, remarried, what the hell.

Someone once wrote that the art of living was a series of give and take, ebb and flow, light and dark, life and death. Keep your expectations under wraps. Otherwise, you're going to be sorely disappointed.

PARIS IS NOTHING like Newark, I thought that first morning in France. Underfoot, one felt the tramp of ages past, the wet clack of heels on stone before the turrets of l'Hotel de Ville. The Beaux Arts apartments along the Seine were large, gray, yet at human scale. I imagined open rooms with floor-to-ceiling windows. The buildings I saw resisted nothing, not the scudding clouds across the sky, not the dreams of restless souls.

"I'm starting to come back," I told M.

"Me, too," she said.

"We could order a coffee, no?"

"We could order a coffee, yes."

It was June in Paris and tourists were everywhere, but a stone's throw from our hotel we found the perfect café. A young Parisian was deep into *Le Monde*, visitors had the good sense to keep *Insight* guides out of sight, waiters cleared tables in a single movement. A gypsy boy was playing folk songs on a squeeze box. Although many of us at the café gave him spare change, he stopped only before M., who had smiled at the child toddling at his side. "Bonne chance," the musician said as he waved goodbye.

Like high school sweethearts, M. and I returned arm-in-arm to the front desk of l'Hotel des Maronniers on rue Jacob, a hidden street in the Latin Quarter. On either side of the little street, five-story apartment buildings drew scant attention to themselves. It was quiet, even peaceful. Never had I been so deliciously tired, so ready for love.

While M. did the check-in, I took the key to our room and went upstairs. I flopped down on the bed and tried to get comfortable but my belt was new and stiff and digging into my side, so I took it off and put it on top of the armoire. Then I unfastened the top buttons of my shirt and lay back on one of four pillows that had been plumped for us. Fresh air filled the room and I took deep, satisfying breaths. The window opened onto a garden of flowering chestnut trees and songbirds; glass-topped dining tables and white chairs stood on crushed stone.

I woke to M. at my side, gently nudging me awake. "Darling, . . ." she said, smiling. Propped up on my elbows, I looked around. The room was big, half the top floor of the country-style hotel; the bed firm but not hard, just the way we liked it.

"Don't you just love the view," I said, reaching for her.

"Yes, dear, I do, but . . ."

"And the light is *magnifique, ne c'est pas?*" I said, rising above her, feeling amorous after my brief rest.

"Yes, . . . but honey, would you mind so terribly if we looked at another room?"

M. traced her hand down the bedspread with a look of disgust. The fabric was a bit coarse, but then I noticed its red brocade, which matched the carpet, the wallpaper, the headboard—even the toilet door. M. had dreamed of just the right room, something country French, charming and elegant, not one that looked as if it belonged in a Turkish bordello. We owed it to ourselves, she said, to insist on the right room.

While I'd slept, the maid had shown M. to a room down the hall. We made our way there and M. hugged and kissed me. "Isn't this much better?" she asked. Hardly, I thought. The room was in an alcove and was small and stuffy. The view to the garden was blocked by a giant tree and the window was half the size of the window in the other room. Worse, we were probably paying the same steep price for a room half as big. But M. seemed so happy that I lacked the heart to argue with her. "It's lovely," I said, then we lay down on the inoffensive bedspread and went to sleep.

It wasn't until I got up from the afternoon nap that I realized I'd left my belt in the other room.

"Don't worry about it, the maid will get it," M. said.

"No, no, my trousers will fall down," I said, knocking on the bordello door. There was no answer. I tried the door but it was locked and we'd also left the key in the room.

"You're right," I agreed finally, "It will get turned in to the front desk. Let's have a good time."

Our hotel manager suggested a restaurant in the style of Toulouse Lautrec that was a favorite of Princess Di, and we savored the antipasti, the carpaccio and parmesan, the homemade wine. We began

wondering whom the lovelorn princess had met secretly at this café—
a ship captain? her chief of staff? an Italian busboy?

My shirt rode up my back as I leaned forward to kiss M. "I
love you," I said. "I'm so glad I waited to see Paris with you. It's a
dream, a dream come true."

That night we fell into each other's arms—and went to sleep. I
awoke at dawn with stomach pangs from the bistro food and took
some medicine. But it was no good, the stomach pressure never let
up. I sat in bed and watched M., sleeping like a baby, curled up in
a ball. All I had to do was reach out and touch her and she would
open to me, hold me tenderly. Instead, I felt sick and uncertain. A
church bell tolled. In the half-light the blue flowers of the wallpaper
looked greenish, mottled, like I imagined my insides to be.

FOR YEARS WHEN I thought of lovemaking I'd go back to that cold
February night twenty-five years ago. The girl I was dating lived in
a nearby town and I was driving her home. That night in the car she
kissed me hard and insisted that I stay.

"But your parents—your brother?" I said. We were eighteen
years old.

"Don't worry about them . . . I love you," she said, pressing the
weight of her body to mine on the cloth bench seat of my father's
Chevrolet.

As quietly as possible, W. and I pulled out the day bed in the
den. Her brother was a bit younger than I, but he'd worked summers
on a farm and was big and strong for his age. His room was directly
above the den. Down the hall from his room was the parents' master
bedroom.

W. was wearing only her panties, the girl-school kind—wide,
round, and bone-white. As my eyes adjusted to the dark, I noticed
her smallish breasts, rising and falling as she lay still on her back.
Her skin was shiny and translucent, like Catherine's in *Wuthering*

Heights. In the car, and again on the front porch, we'd kissed and groped at each other in a frenzy. Now, in this bed beside her, I lay on my back, staring at the ceiling, at the piano, at a forest landscape on the wall. Again and again, I rose on top of her. But it was no use. On the day bed in the den of my girlfriend's father's house, I couldn't do a thing. I lay awake for an hour or two, then left her sleeping, stole out the door, and drove home.

THE BELT WAS not at the front desk the next morning, and the clerks were adamant: they could not remove anything from the room without the permission of the new guests. M. pulled at my hand, told me to forget it, we could find another belt. "Uh huh," I said, looking past her as I wrote in my journal.

During our frequent travels together writing in our journals has become our way of setting the stage for intimacy. If we each have an hour or two to write, to work on our novels, bits of stories, or magazine assignments, then in the afternoon we can be together, go for long walks, make love.

"What are you working on?" M. asked after breakfast in the hotel courtyard.

I turned the journal toward her and she read:

OCCUPANTS OF ROOM 53

Please forgive the intrusion. Before I took up occupancy in Room 51, I had for a brief time been an occupant of your room and left my belt behind on top of the closet. Could you be so kind as to retrieve it and leave the belt for me at the front desk.

Sincerely,
Occupant of Room 51

"A touch too formal, don't you think?" M. said with more than a trace of sarcasm as she handed the journal back to me.

"Maybe, but I think it will work," I said with a wink. M. was laughing to herself as I swept by her, rushing to put the page I'd ripped from my journal under the door of our former room.

French coins were heavy in my pockets and with every step I took that morning in Paris, I was afraid my trousers would fall down. In the Musee d'Orsée, my briefs showed. We asked a tourist to take our photo by the Eiffel Tower; with one arm I hugged M. to me while the other was holding up my waistband. I'd arrange myself at cafés, prepared to write in my journal, but I couldn't concentrate. "C'mon, let's go," I said finally, pulling M. in and out of mens' stores in the Latin Quarter, where ordinary-looking belts were going for one hundred dollars. We couldn't afford that; we were stretching our finances as it was.

Near the end of the day we stopped at the front desk of our hotel before going upstairs. No belt.

"It was your fault you forgot the belt," M. said "If you hadn't been so careless. . . ."

"There was nothing wrong with the other room," I blurted, jumping to my feet. "There was light, a breeze, a beautiful view."

"Why didn't you tell me that then?" she snapped. "Why don't you ever tell me what you feel?"

"I was showing you, damn it! I wanted to make love in that room. With you!"

I glared at her, thought for the first time in my life that if I could get my hands on a belt I would thrash her with it. Then, suddenly feeling faint, I collapsed on the bed. I had waited a lifetime for Paris, the city of love, of Balzac, the place where Henry Miller, a hero of my youth, set down the wisdom of the heart.

"If you hadn't wanted to change rooms," I said, barely above a whisper.

"Perhaps if we tried some stores in the outskirts, the prices would be affordable," she suggested.

Yes, I agreed, that was a good idea. We caught a bus, but it didn't seem to get anywhere. *La Petite Ceinture*, the route was called. The Little Belt.

AS FAR AS my friends were concerned, I'd lost my virginity that night on the day bed in W.'s father's den. The only part I would leave out as I told the story again and again was how we never really did it. I'd get to that part and smile, blush, shrug. Guys clapped me on the back to hear about how I had landed in W.'s day bed, a pullout couch in her father's den. If you're going to do it for the first time that was the place, said the school quarterback, socking my shoulder. I told myself that such a lie was harmless, just a matter of going along to get along and would have no lasting effect on me.

But for years after the sexless night on the day bed with W., I didn't sleep with a woman. Whenever it came to the moment of decision, I backed off, said, no, no, talked in my fake Robert Redford voice about my respect for a woman's honor. I had decided that I was saving myself, waiting for the woman whom I truly loved. Half-truths about love sculpt the foundations of a guy's social rites and codes of honor—there were my own expectations about love and the potential for love, but the expectations of my peers, too.

In looking back I suppose that it was true that the young women I was seeing were often not right for me. But the greater truth was that I was scared of real intimacy, of exposing the petty lies I was telling myself and the people close to me. When telling lies becomes not only easy but a part of you, what chance does love have?

THAT NIGHT AS M. slept, I was up, my mind racing as it hadn't since I was a teenager. But instead of thinking about girls, sports, and cars, I imagined the standing water collecting on the roof of our first-floor addition, the flaking brick facade from our brownstone which needed pointing. How was K. holding up at Grandma's, the dog at Gordon's?

I dreamed that I was walking the streets of Paris. I was hungry and needy and looking for a place to eat and rest. As I moved through the city, I recognized the stores, the people, and not in some superficial way. With each step I felt more connected to the city, but with increasing anxiety. The streets themselves were spinning in circles; one street was indistinguishable from the next. Paris is circular, spherical, like the workings of the brain and the intestines. One either feels the pressure of the bowels or the brain.

I awoke in a cold sweat and stayed awake until dawn. M. was sleeping at the corner of the bed.

Paris was slipping away from me.

AT BREAKFAST THE third morning a thin man walked by with a smartly dressed companion. His double-breasted sports jacket was strategically closed, snugly buttoned at his waist. Not only was I convinced that this man had taken my belt, but in my sleep-deprived state I was certain he was wearing it under his expensive coat.

If not him, then there was this other man, a German car salesman with a pasty face. But he didn't wear my belt out of doors. He preferred to model it for his wife before the mirror, putting it back where he got it, on top of the armoire. Or the genteel English fatherly type on the fourth floor. Who would suspect him?

I'd toyed with the idea of staking out our former room, dressed in a loud shirt and holding a brochure to the Louvre. By seeming nonchalant and waiting for my prey to come bounding out the door, I could catch him red-handed. But if the man could steal, would he be shamed into admitting the crime? It was his word against mine.

The next day the Occupants of Room 53 checked out before we woke up. We asked the maid to search the room. No belt. I imagined a man taking the belt down from the armoire, fingering the fine leather, the designer clasp. Then, into the garment bag, zip, snap, gone. My belt would travel on to Frankfurt, Rome, Copenhagen— to other trips and adventures—while I would soon be heading home, wondering where we would find the money to fix the roof.

ON OUR FIRST date I drove M. in my un-airconditioned car in one hundred degree weather to a suburban movie plaza to watch *Bull Durham*, the baseball movie. Hot air poured through the open windows as M. took off her sandals and put her bare feet on the dash. Her sundress flapped in the wind of the moving car, and we talked and joked—about what, I don't remember. I remember only how right that moment felt, of how I was beginning to fall in love with her. Something inside me was giving way, and I found myself talking freely about my feelings as I hadn't in years. M. remembers only that I didn't take her hand, that I didn't touch her in any way, not in the car, the dark of the movie, or in the parking lot afterward. She was convinced that I was gay.

But then we began to do everything together. We were attending a writers' conference in Richmond, Virginia, and after classes we toured the historic capitol buildings, visited Poe's House, marveled at the antebellum grandeur of the Jefferson Hotel. At parties, we moved among strangers with the ease of a happy couple celebrating an anniversary. Even before our second date, I had helped her with her wash, folded her warm, intimate things with mine. When we visited Hollywood Cemetery we didn't see the graves of Jefferson Davis and John Munro, we followed the antics of two mad squirrels and laughed as they tumbled over each other in the heavy heat. Sex was passionate and tender, not like anything either of us could ever remember in a long time.

At the end of a day near the close of the conference, I bought a dozen candles and arranged them around M.'s room when she was out. I lit the candles, put a rose in a vase, chilled some wine. When she returned, M. stared hard at me for a beat, then turned aside the glass of wine. "It's all going a bit too fast for me," she said, her eyes glowering. We argued bitterly and that night was the first night in a week we did not make love.

For hours I wrote in my journal, the unlit candles surrounding me. In a broken-down car rattling through the warehouse district of a faceless city, I'd fallen in love with a woman. On our second date we'd attended an exhibit on slavery. Giant reproductions on beige backdrops depicted colonial drawings of heroic figures at a slave auction; a single video image of crude leg shackles accompanied an explanation, "Some slaves remained in the home." We were repulsed and amazed, stirred to anger, then, in exasperation, laughter. I knew that intimacy was built by a steady stream of tiny measures, not by grand, set-piece gestures. But I couldn't let go. By setting up the big expectation I inevitably found myself back on the day bed in W.'s father's house, forever trying to make it right, to make love with the beautiful girl I'd lost so long ago. And like that night a quarter century ago I would try and try again but never succeed.

I left Richmond that summer weekend not knowing if I would ever see M. again. We were living in different cities then and for what seemed like a long time we didn't speak. Finally, we did begin to see each other and a year later we were married before a few friends and family. But aside from bringing home flowers and the occasional theater ticket, I rarely lay in wait for love.

Paris was only confirming what I already knew, what I somehow couldn't bring myself to admit. In my life, plans for love always fell flat.

THE AFTERNOON OF our fourth day in Paris, M. and I stopped at an open-air market to buy some cheese, fruit, and a bottle of wine for a picnic at the Luxembourg Gardens. Marie de Medici had guaranteed the beauty of this public space more than 370 years ago when she prevailed upon her husband, Henry IV, to improve the plumbing. He had to repair and reopen the old Gallo-Roman aqueduct to do so, and fourteen fountains had to be built to carry off the excess water. Marie's gardens were the reward. I felt M.'s eyes on me as I was telling the story, carting the bag of food and drink in one hand, holding up my trousers in another.

Then a straight-backed man in a safari suit loped into view carrying at arm's length an oversized map. He was wearing a wide-brimmed safari hat, with a thick scarf wrapped about his neck like a rainforest snake. A Montgomery Clift lookalike, oblivious to the crowds of tourists and fashionable Parisian couples on their lunch breaks, the safari man high-stepped his way through the gardens in as straight a line as he could manage.

"Looking for Livingston, I presume," I said.

M. laughed and in the dappled light under the chestnut tree she looked beautiful. We arranged two chairs in the shade as a man and a boy approached us for food. They both looked tired and wan, and M. pulled two peaches from our bag and gave them each one. The man returned the peach given to him, but accepted the gift for his son with a smile before walking on. I touched M.'s cheek and she moved toward me and we kissed. Then I lifted her from the chair and from our knees we continued kissing under the chestnut tree. I'd learned as a boy there's a place in the small of the back where in a northern winter the cold settles. The trick is to relax that spot and release the warmth. It seemed funny to think of that then, while kissing M. on the grass in the Luxembourg Gardens, but I did and such heat as I couldn't remember washed over me.

Then M. offered me the peach. As I reached forward to take a bite, I noticed the leaves of the chestnut tree as they rustled in the breeze. Shafts of sunlight danced on the ground. There were many people in the garden that day, but I don't remember hearing their voices, only the sound of the fountains, the steady splash of water. I took a bite of the peach M. held in her hand. It tasted sweet. Juice dribbled onto M.'s hand and down her wrist. It was the best peach I'd ever eaten. I licked juice from M.'s arm and then held the peach out to her and she tasted it too.

"WHAT'S NEXT?"

MICKEY PEARLMAN

EVERY YEAR ON their wedding anniversary my distinguished starched-white-shirt and bowtied father, the attorney, sent my artistic and intellectually frustrated mother, the sculptor, a dozen long-stemmed American Beautys. On the card were written these words: "Love sends a little gift of roses."

And she hated it, as only a redheaded, green-eyed vamp from Savannah could. She hated the roses, the card, the very dependability and expectedness of it all, and I sensed even as a small child that what she was reacting against was the sameness, the stretching before her of years of quaint southern romanticism and dignified love. I, on the other hand, loved it, loved the gallantry and the optimism of this vision—that all could be put right by a luxurious bouquet.

For my mother this was just one more time when she did not have to say the words, "What's next?" Trapped in a comfortable cocoon, she *knew* what was coming next and she was bored almost out of her southern mind with that knowledge.

That was, of course, (many years later) before my father wasn't there to meet her train the day she returned from the baths in Hot Springs, Arkansas. She found him, dressed in the starched white shirt, his polished oxfords waiting near his feet, in his favorite chair—dead of a massive heart attack. That was, of course, (many years later) before my 51-year-old brother went in for an angiogram and his heart exploded in the operating room.

That was what was next. So it's probably a very good thing that she didn't ask.

LAST YEAR AS I held the icy hand of my best friend as she lay dying (even that body part suffused with cancer), I thought to myself, "Now here is a woman who *always* asked 'What's next?'" She said it every time her preferred Democratic left wing was bloodied as if the monster Grendel were chewing on the heart of Beowulf, she said it whenever a former or current student was drugged out or arrested, she asked that question after every decimation of the powerless by the powerful, and after every failure of hope over experience. "What's next?" was her mantra—as if repeating it could ward off the unbidden realities that this high school English teacher did not want to absorb into her increasingly crowded memory bank.

Like all extraordinary humans she was intensely complicated and contradictory. While she could get more joy out of a concert at Tanglewood or a doubleheader at Yankee Stadium (even in the cheap seats), or a forty-buck win on her weekly lottery ticket than anyone, there seemed always to be a shadow over her head, the legacy of too many stories about the ten babies that had died in her grandmother's womb, planes that dropped from the sky, the fishbone in the throat— all a residue of the (realistic) anxiety that many people from the working class have about staying afloat. And in thirty-five years of friendship this functioned as our major point of tension. I didn't want to hear, in our weekly Sunday morning phone calls, about how what's-her-name's sister-in-law's cousin, four times removed, had been hit by a meteor in Sheboygan, or the five newest theories disseminating among her students about how the (pick one) Jews, Irish,

Italians, mainline Chinese, or Haitians had introduced the AIDS virus to Harlem and the political implications thereof. I saw all of this as the curse of the committed pessimist, ready for her quotidian dose of salt tears, the hallmark of someone who was not fully conscious of her affinity for bad news, who didn't understand her commitment to the idea that something bad was just about to happen. (The congregation will say in unison: it did.) I suppose that I can see it now—retrospect, as always, giving us a second shot at some kind of wisdom—as her hand raised against the devil, as her Bronx cheer against the evil eye.

To put it simply, she expected complications and she prepared for them like the good soldier she was: bills paid on time, expensive snow tires, money socked away for retirement, regular paint and cleaning sessions on an already spotless residence. And although the black cloud hovered over her sightline she believed to her dying day in the goodness of possibility and the possibility of goodness. While I and most of her "intellectual" friends were ranting that Spanish had perhaps become the national language of certain parts of the USA, she took a sabbatical and learned Spanish. (As she would have said, *"Hell-oo?"* translation: *wake up to reality.*) While the rest of us were throwing up our hands at the right wing leadership in Washington, she was running around New York City, scrounging scholarship funding for every minority student at her high school in Queens and sending them off, one by one, like unpaired animals marching into an ark, to Cornell, Dartmouth, and Smith. She lived her politics, this woman; she hung tough.

And she definitely believed in love, although she never married or had children of her own. (Of course almost everyone's children, including mine, would have chosen her for the primary parent had there been a vote.) So, she spent some of her passion on Tennyson, and on the magical realism of García Márquez, drawn to him, no doubt, by the utopian vision and the dystopian reality. No one who studied *Macbeth* with her ever forgot the "out, damned spot" scene. (She hid opened McDonald's catsup packets under her cuffs and the red stuff shot out at the appropriate moment.) She loved the "centering experience" of the beach, and the commotion of Thanksgiving. Can someone with two master's degrees love the slot machines in Vegas? I think so; it's the perfect place for a "What's next?" kind of gal.

A FORMER MENTOR once told me that "you learn who you are from who you're not." I realize that my friend's pessimism annoyed me precisely because it got in the way of my own style, described best as the no problemo, suck it up, get-over-it approach of the New Jerseyan I had become. And I had enough trouble with the familiar cynicism of other friends who were never surprised by anything but *good* news. After all, I had been raised to believe that love not only sends a little gift of roses, but that it acts as some sort of magical laminate that Scotchguards the bodies and souls of the beloved. I suppose I had unconsciously come to believe in what the pop psychologists lamely call the power of love. You love the right people, love protects them, no cancer invades; no hearts explode. Simple. (It's not, but this view is so comforting that even now it's hard to give up. Was my brain baked by the southern sun during all those childhood hours spent practicing baton twirling in the park?)

The writer Dennis McFarland reminded me recently that in Eastern philosophies they don't say "What's next?" They ask, "What's now?" I wish I'd remembered this from a long-ago course in Comparative Religions. I only remember that my professor was a poultry farmer in his other life and he talked about ugly ducklings and beautiful profits more than he explained the teachings of Siddhartha Gautama, the *Bhagavad-Gita* or the *Upanishads.*

Had he gotten around to "What's now?" I might have understood sooner that for everyone the great epiphany of middle age—

which for me *is* what's now—is not only that your estrogen or tes-
tosterone levels drop, or that your body parts seem to rearrange themselves in a less felicitous configuration, or that hair thins and teeth
chip. The real news is that love becomes so often intertwined with
loss, sometimes of the very people whom you expected to bury you,
and of the older generation. A writer friend whose mother recently
died wrote to me the other day and said that she was "making [her]
way ever so carefully from the life I had with a mother to the life
I'm going to have without one."

Burying your friends and the love objects of your childhood
leaves both empty spaces and unanswered questions. If I have no
parents, am I still a daughter? If I have no aunts or uncles, am I still
a niece? When, if ever, will my heart heal after the loss of my wonderful friend? What is the sound of one hand clapping? What's next?
What's now?

I think of all the discussions I had with one of the three central
figures of my childhood, the prototype for the "What's now?"
woman, who died a few years ago at 93. My aunt was the mother
of three, the oldest of whom, a 30-year-old son, was killed when the
driver of the truck in which he was riding tried to cross the tracks
in front of an approaching train. The train won, even though this
cousin had served with gutsiness on Guadacanal in World War II.
Since all of this took place in Israel almost fifty years ago, before the
days of computerized records, fax machines, and international policies
on recovered corpses, we waited for six weeks before the body was
returned to her in a lead-sealed coffin enclosed in an elongated orange
crate.

What's next? What's now? I don't think she asked. I do remember that her response to loss was to throw out most of the rules, to
carpe diem as well as someone who was born in 1897 and raised in
the deep South could manage to do. She made her own rules: only
wear "real" jewelry, always have some money that no one else knows

about (a *knippel*), and buy *only* expensive perfume, preferably from France.

All of us cousins clustered at her house although she could only "cook" three things (if you count salad made from canned salmon) and certainly did not have the most room for unruly children armed with tennis rackets, etudes to practice, and French verbs to memorize. (My nursemaid, Ida Mae Simmons, once told me, "Mickey Lou, all the wrong people have extra bedrooms," and she was prescient in that wisdom.) We pushed the overstuffed Morris chairs of the 1950s together to make beds, regularly raided the closet where the *National Geographics* were stacked on a high shelf (Wow! naked breasts, almost see-able penises!), and took bubble baths in small groups. My aunt threw the girls' underpants in the tub with us and they floated every night among the bodies. I can remember how "disgusting" my mother thought this was but even then people had different rapprochements with joie de vivre.

My aunt could get a lot of mileage out of what seems in our jaded time to be insignificant pleasures. One of those pleasures was her "peruke," a long thatch of silky human hair, attached to a comb, that lived between wearings on the doorknob of her dressing-room closet. It was my job every morning to unhook it from its resting place and to brush it into wearability before it was bobbypinned onto my aunt's remaining hair and then wound into a towering tiara. What are the implications of dressing up like a queen every morning? Was this optimism contagious? What did this teach me about love? That the ghosts can also come to the party; that the only unguent for loss *is* love. That in the end love is nothing more or less than optimism, even when it is sometimes couched in pessimism, and that love always has its way with the lover and the loved.

AN ACQUAINTANCE AND I were discussing death the other day and she remarked that by this time I "must have become an expert in grieving," as if anyone would want to earn money for accumulated sadness in a poker game where you ante up resiliance. I looked at her as if she were nuts (no proper psychoanalytical word presented itself here) or as if she were a visitor from a less complicated planet. No, I said, "I am no expert in grieving; I just try to find a place in my head for whatever happens, and I suppose that when all the space is filled up it will be time to check out."

That will be, you might say, what's next.

FIRST LOVE

JOYCE CAROL OATES

I will analyze the actions and appetites of men as if it were a question of lines, of planes, and of solids.

—SPINOZA

I

... A VOICE OF logic, reason, conviction, irony; a low, throaty, musical voice; a seductive voice; an arrogant voice; a young, impetuous voice; a voice of occasional hesitation, uncertainty; a voice that provoked, annoyed, beset; a shrewd voice; a voice of humility; a voice sharp as a knife blade; a voice like warm butter; a voice I would have wished for myself if I'd been born *male* and not *female*; a voice I did in fact wish for myself though born not *male* but *female*; a voice that by degrees had so seeped into my consciousness that it began to emerge, in the late winter of my second year at the university, in my most vivid, ravaging, and exhausting dreams.

Author's note: "First Love" an excerpt from the novel *The Negro-Lover*, is a minute examination of that intense and obsessive state of consciousness called "infatuation" or "romantic love." The genre to which it belongs might be defined as "fiction-memoir."

He lived in the most ordinary of places: a second-floor rear apartment in an ugly cube of a stucco apartment building at 1183 Chambers Street, Syracuse, New York. In a neighborhood down behind the university hospital, an old neighborhood in the very shadow of new high-rise buildings and multi-leveled parking lots; a place of stucco and cinderblock apartment buildings and aging woodframe houses partitioned into rooms for older university students, many of them foreign students. Chambers Street was steeply hilly, the pavement cracked and potholed. Most of the curbside elms had been cut down, blighted by Dutch elm disease. Yet here was a place of fascination and romance, greedily I'd memorized the rain-streaked facade of the building at 1183 Chambers, the perennial sign APTS FOR RENT INQUIRE WITHIN; the rotted-shingled roof and drainpipes choked with leaves; the fractured concrete walk leading to the front entrance and forking around the side of the building to a flight of outdoor steps that led to the second floor; this outdoor, covered stairway of raw planks crudely painted to match the mustard-yellow stucco. *I am just passing by, on my way somewhere else.* Yet a mile or more from my own residence on the far side of the sprawling university campus. Passing his building twice, three times; walking quickly, eyes averted; not knowing if he was home, unless it was twilight, or dark, and his windows were unlighted; not knowing if at any moment he might return home, on foot like me, in danger of seeing me—whom he might, or might not recognize. Sometimes I turned into the narrow, trash-littered alley beside his apartment building, passing close by the outdoor stairway; *his* stairway (shared with several other tenants, dark-skinned foreign students); I saw that dogs had dragged garbage out of overturned trash cans; I gazed at the windows at the rear of the building that were *his*; for somehow I'd found out which windows were *his* (belonging to apartment 2D); which blinds, infrequently drawn and luridly stained and cracked when drawn, were *his*. And sometimes his shadow, the silhouette of his very body, defined against the blind . . . *And his not knowing I am here, never guessing.*

Yet it was more risky, thus more exciting, for me to contemplate his windows during the day, when I couldn't be sure he was not home; and if he was, how easy for him to look out, and see—*me*.

That look in my face of raw female yearning: *love me*.

Never would I have dared climb the stairway, never dared knock at the door of 2D; this would have been a violation of Vernor Matheius's privacy, dignity. (And yet: there were confused, anguished, sexually aroused dreams in which I did just that, and was admitted to his apartment; yet the man who opened the door, drew me in, was a faceless stranger, his skin vaporous and no-color, and not *him*.) It was enough for me to know that he lived alone; had he lived with a woman, a girl, had he been married, I would have despaired; my fantasies would have been rooted in despair, and not in hope; he was a graduate student presumably in his late twenties (though possibly older) and might easily have been married like so many graduate students of the era, might easily have had small children like the harassed couples who lived in the university's barracks-style housing amid a squalor of overturned tricycles, wagons, children's broken toys. *This is the consequence of romance, love, sexual desire: the new, ever-burgeoning generation.* Yet I did not think of such things, I would not have wished to connect my fantasies of yearning and exultation with so blunt, so obvious a principle; this would have seemed to me vulgar, demeaning; unworthy of my adoration of Vernor Matheius.

Nor did I think *So this is it: love*. I did not think *At last you are normal, a female like the others*. I did not feel the relief tinged with sickness, faintness, embarrassment I'd felt at the age of fourteen when I'd recognized the first earthy-red blood smears in the crotch of my pajamas that meant menstruation. (Yet more than merely menstruation: female normality. For despite my pride I yearned above all things to be *normal.*) I did not connect my condition, the madness of my condition, with anything that might be shared with or even comprehended by others; I would not have wished for solace; when I was too restless to concentrate on my studies, to stay in one place, to sleep, I left my residence hall to make my way a mile or more beyond the university medical buildings down a steep hill and up another in the glacier-mutilated landscape I had come by degrees to love; since falling in love; as if "love" had festered in me for nearly nineteen years (since my mother had died) and now that I was in love with the man, Vernor Matheius, with whom I was in love, or believed myself in love, "love" welled up inside me like a subterranean spring. Lush, promiscuous, unstoppable. I would drown in it!

One morning in late February finding myself again as in a dream of repetition, compulsion, enchantment ... in the trash-littered alley beside 1183 Chambers Street gazing at the tracery of fresh-fallen snow on the roof, the hieroglyphic patterns of snow driven into the stucco; it was a bright blazing day following a night of exhausting half-sleep; sunshine like a shout of God to wake us; I did not believe in God as others seemed to believe yet I understood why one might believe; my eyes flooded with an inexpressible gratitude. *I owe everything to him, he has wakened me, made my life possible.* I had a premonition that, at any minute, he would appear. If I waited, he would suddenly come down the outdoor stairway, hurrying, he was always in a hurry, frowning to himself, his round wire-rimmed eyeglasses glinting, he would be wearing the khaki-colored sheepskin jacket, a crimson wool scarf looped about his neck, he would be wearing hiking boots, carrying himself with one shoulder just perceptibly raised, the left shoulder higher than the right and his head at a slight angle as if brooding, lost in thought. I was in terror of being seen; yet in greater terror of not being seen; I would wait ten minutes, or fifteen, and no longer; until in fact a man hurried down the stairs—dark-skinned, diminutive, an Indian or a Pakistani graduate student, and not Vernor Matheius—not *him*. And shortly afterward there came a man along the alley, an elderly white man walking a dog, a retired professor he seemed to me, though it seemed unlikely that a retired professor would be living in this rundown neighborhood behind the hospital; he was squinting at me as if he hoped he might know me, or I might know him; I smiled saying hello, what a beautiful day, and he smiled eagerly, tipping his hat and smiling, "Beautiful day, yes isn't it? After all."

Together we watched as his short-legged thick-bodied wheezing terrier sniffed at a patch of yellow-splotched snow.

3

Who is that, what kind of person is that? Almost I'd felt a stab of fear.

The voice. The voice like no other voice I'd ever heard. Before I knew his name or had even glimpsed him: located him. Before I'd been able to say *So that is the man: him.*

At the age of nineteen I had no interest in any man, or in maleness; I was disdainful of maleness, or so I believed; it was purely intelligence I admired, whether in men or in women, and I had found none in women, in my personal experience. I was studying philosophy because it promised, if not truth, a rigorous and unsentimental quest for truth; a field of knowledge that was also a way of being, a methodology for life. *What is it?* philosophy asks. *Who are you, of what substance are you? And why? To what end?*

I was enrolled in an upper-division course in ethics, which was offered to both undergraduates and graduate students; the class met three times a week on the fourth, topmost floor of an antiquated building called the Hall of Languages; at the end of his lecture, the professor invited questions from students, and was clearly enlivened when one or another of the older students volunteered to speak. *He* was one of them. "Yes, Mr.—" the professor would say, pronouncing a name that resembled "math"—"mathes"—which I couldn't quite hear. The young man sat at the very rear of the lecture hall and often had a question, or a comment to make; hearing him, I had to resist turning like the others, who stared in curiosity, surprise, admiration, resentment; I thought too well of myself and of my own dense and convoluted thought to appear to think well of another's. "How can Plato promote the strategy of the 'noble lie,' " demanded the voice from the back of the room, "—as if any lie is anything other than ignoble!" And the professor smiled, a rather worn smile, and said defensively, "The entire *Republic* is a metaphor, a myth, it's best understood as a dialogue about justice," and he at the back of the room, incensed now, raising his voice in revulsion, "Some 'justice'! Plato's utopia is a nightmare fascist state." And the professor persevered, stammering slightly, not at all liking it that he was losing the allegiance of the class to an interloper thirty years his junior, "Now, that's a common fallacy, Mr. M—. What should be kept in mind. . . ." But few of us were listening to the professor, we were listening solely to *him.*

I remember the curious proportions of that room, that drafty lecture hall, as we remember any space in which our lives have been irrevocably altered. There were fifteen rows of seats in steeply rising tiers that curved far to each side in the shape of a crescent, so that the room was much wider than it was deep. The ceiling was extremely high, and water-stained; fluorescent tubing hummed and quivered overhead like racing thoughts.

One morning following the professor's lecture on the topic of philosophic idealism, there was a lengthy exchange between the professor and the highly articulate young man at the back of the hall; I felt a collective wave of dislike, directed toward the young man; others turned to gape, but I did not: though I listened, in fascination; excitement and apprehension: thinking *Who is that, what kind of person is that? Like no one of us.* Behind me a male voice muttered sullenly, "Oh for Christ's sake shut up," and another what sounded like "N'ggg shut yo mouth," and both laughed unkindly. By this time the professor was speaking defensively and at length; he would punish the entire class by keeping us beyond the end of the hour. I thought *We should not have such power over one another.* When finally the class dispersed I was slow to rise to my feet, and to stumble into the aisle; still I had not allowed myself to look at the back of the room; I did not yet understand that I was in love; I'd fallen in love with a man I did not know; with a man's mere voice; and that love is a kind of illness; not a radiant idea as I'd imagined but a physical condition, like grief.

That night in early February 1963 was the first night his voice entered my sleep.

4

You are capable of any thing my brother Hendrick once told me.

Any thing: how strange the words, the usage. For he'd said it quite clearly: *any thing* and not *anything*: as if that of which I was capable was a thing and not an action.

Yet Hendrick had no idea of that which I was capable, nor did anyone in my family; of course, I had no idea, myself. I was nineteen years old and five months when I fell in love for the first time in my life; a profound, advanced age to me; yet to my disgust I appeared much younger. In my clumsy winter boots—not chic leather of the kind worn by the better-dressed college girls, these were hardy "rubberized" boots from Sears—I stood no taller than five feet three inches. My weight was ninety-five pounds. My body (did I possess a body? or was it as Descartes had fantasized, a mysterious and unknowable substance constituted my mind, and an entirely other mysterious and unknowable substance constituted my body?) was that of a mildly malnourished thirteen-year-old girl with slender bones, papery-thin tallow-colored skin stretched tight. My breasts were the size of Dixie cups and stony-hard; the nipples were the size of wizened peas, lacking the warm roseate aureole, the purplish-fruity texture of those girls' breasts I presumed to be "normal": the heavier, fuller breasts of other girls my age which looked as if already they held liquid, a sweet milky precious liquid, and could not possibly be hard and ungiving as my own. These breasts I'd shyly glimpsed in school showers or locker rooms, as early as seventh grade, when I would glance at a partially undressed girl and then quickly away as if I'd seen a forbidden sight. Where other girls stared boldly, or laughed and made jokes, peeling off their outer clothes, removing sweaters in a single flamboyant gesture that exposed their torsos even as their heads and faces were obscured for a swift magical moment, where others stood defiant or proud or supremely indifferent in their burgeoning bodies, I turned away in embarrassment; it was not that I felt inferior or inadequate in my spindly body, I would not have compared myself with other girls at all, no more than I would have compared myself with an adult woman—the billboard, movie-poster, television images of female beauty and glamor. I stood outside their category entirely, a marginal subspecies of *girl.*

My face was small, oval, severe with vivid features like a face in a pen-and-ink drawing by Matisse; my eyes were deep-set and large, unnaturally shiny and dark—all pupil. There had been girl friends and well-intentioned female relatives who'd gently chided *If you would smile, not frown*—their voices trailing off with cryptic meaning; and I'd been cut to the heart, thinking furiously *But I am smiling, can't you see I am smiling constantly? I'm laughing in your faces!*

I didn't want their pity, their sympathy or solicitude. I knew that they felt sorry for me because they took pleasure in feeling sorry for one so handicapped, so disfigured because I had no mother, no living mother, alone of the girls of my generation in Strykersville where I'd grown up I had no mother; sometimes it seemed to my horror that my mother had died before I'd been born; if such a legend could be, it would apply to me—*the girl whose mother died before she was born*. Growing up I had had only stubborn, secret memories of my mother which I would share with no one; and these memories, un-shared, had grown aged, brittle, cracked, and crumbling like yellowed old pages hoarded close to my body, my small stony-hard breasts that would never yield milk to any sucking mouth. Motherless I determined *I would require no mother* and so it came to be. And there were my three tall beautiful brothers whom I'd adored all my life, my brothers who were many years older than I and naturally had no time or patience for me; except sometimes to tease, chide, whistle *Hey Babe!* or *Little Puss!* or *Sour-puss!* or *Sex-y!* scarcely glancing at me. My grandmother (my father's mother) hoped to console me saying my brothers loved me, of course they loved me but didn't know how to show it, men rarely know how to show love; and I said bitterly, the taste like acid in my mouth *Who wants their love? Who wants love? Love makes you weak, love causes you to die* (as my mother had died). *I don't need love from any of you!* And perhaps I believed it, this curse; perhaps it was even true; there may have been brotherly affection in their tor-ment of me but I felt only torment, not affection. I would feel it all my life, I would never forgive them as I would never forgive my mother for abandoning me when I was eighteen months old and I would never forgive my father for abandoning me all my life, and for dying. From my brothers' careless laughing talk about girls and women I learned that the male is all eyes; assesses through the eyes; judges you swiftly and without mercy. Sometimes, laughing crudely, speaking of a girl or a woman, my brothers would rub their crotches gleefully. I understood that a man's eyes and his penis are connected, perhaps identical; except the one is slyly hidden from view.

Even when the male is by himself (I thought) he is with other males and his swift pitiless judgment is a collective male judgment.

He has the power to see with others' eyes, not merely his own. And I did not expect mercy from those eyes. Already by the age of thirteen I knew to shrink from their eviscerating gaze.

5

His name was Vernor Matheius.

How many times then I would fall into a trance writing VERNOR MATHEIUS VERNOR MATHEIUS in midnight-blue ink with a fountain pen; sometimes tracing VERNOR MATHEIUS VERNOR MATHEIUS with a sharp fingernail digging into my flesh, the soft inside of my forearm, the palm of my hand. Even in the presence of others, smiling and nodding and talking quite normally with others, in secret I would be tracing VERNOR MATHEIUS VERNOR MATHEIUS: a name, a code, a sound, an incantation mysterious as a riddle out of a Grimm's fairy tale that might have a happy ending, an ending involving a wedding, or might end in doom, death, a nightmare: a naive and ignorant young girl is given magic words to decipher and naturally cannot.

I had boldly inquired among the older students in the ethics class what was the name of the young man at the back of the room, not caring if they reported back to him, as no doubt they did, smiling over me. *See that girl? Asking about you, your name.* And possibly Vernor Matheius had seen me—or possibly not.

Now when the professor called upon "Mr. Matheius" I heard the name perfectly; and wondered how I'd ever misheard it: *Matheius.*

I looked *Vernor Matheius* up in the university directory and now knew his telephone number (which I would never dial) and his address on Chambers Street, a considerable distance from my residence hall *but I would have no trouble walking it* even as I instructed myself *You will never go to 1183 Chambers Street, you will never be so reckless.*

I believed this. I was not deceiving myself.

6

It was an ordinary March morning when I first dared to speak to Vernor Matheius, and entered his life.

By this time I had several times walked to Chambers Street and passed his house; and lingered in the alley; and drifted away again like a lost dog. Even as I understood I was behaving absurdly, I had become a person whom I myself would ridicule; and it seemed quite just, that I'd become this person; I was both an object of ridicule and the one who ridicules; I'd discovered a strange satisfaction in such an anomaly. *You are capable of any thing* was now a prophecy, an encouragement, and not an insult. Of course I had left my seat in the third row of the lecture hall, directly in the field of the professor's gaze, to sit nearer the back of the room; nearer to *him*; in such a position, like any lovesick high school girl, where I could see the object of my adoration without being overly conspicuous. Or so I believed. I'd moved from my original seat not caring that the professor would surely notice; he knew my name and my work, and had praised my work in a previous course as rarely (it was said) he praised undergraduate work and virtually never work by women. And yet I'd heedlessly abandoned my identity in the professor's eyes; I'd jeopardized his good opinion of me; for all men are vain and quick to notice such abrupt switches in female attentiveness. Yet, had I any choice?

This I remember so vividly: climbing the three flights of stairs to the lecture hall, entering the cavernous room breathless and hopeful; it would be several minutes before the start of the class and I would seem to step into a space of vertiginous unease; the entrance was at the rear of the hall, the tiers of seats fanning out far to each side; a roaring seemed to lift out of the room; there was an air of faintness and excitement that (I was certain) was not brought with me but awaited me there, rushing at me like the wind. For what if *he* was already there?—if *he* might glance casually at me, the lenses of his round, metal-rimmed glasses winking like sparks of flame? Usually Vernor Matheius was not already in the room; I wanted always to precede him, to position myself close by the seat that was his customary seat, yet not too close, so that I could watch him without fear of being noticed. The back row of the lecture hall was mostly empty, and he sat, alone, in the center; beneath an old-fashioned wall clock with plain black numerals and slender black hands on a white moon face, how strange that this was the identical clock of my rural grade school at whose black minute hand I would stare fascinated, hypnotized waiting for it to jump, to mark the next minute, always the next minute, and the minute beyond that, forever, and ever!—the black hand jumping to mark the next minute whether I saw or not; measuring the inexorable passage of time I understood even as a child to be my own inexorable heartbeat yet, so unfairly, not in my possession. So that, seeing Vernor Matheius, I was also seeing the clock; glancing back to see the time, I was also seeing Vernor Matheius; the two are inextricably melded in my memory, belonging to that idyllic period of time so like childhood itself before we actually met, touched.

Vividly I remember: taking notes during the lecture like the good-girl student I assuredly was yet under the cover of leaning my head against my hand, my fingers to my forehead and letting my hair fall into my face, how slyly I would watch Vernor Matheius; how dreamily I would gaze at the man's face that seemed to me radiantly beautiful (though it may have been, to another's eyes, radiantly ugly); a strange face, a mask-like face, a thought-crinkled face, a young-old face, flattish nose and deep wide nostrils and full, fleshy lips the color of a bruised plum; eyes hidden behind the lenses of his wire-rimmed glasses except when he removed the glasses to rub the bridge of his nose slowly with the thumb and forefinger of his right hand. At these moments I stared at him openly; his sharp-boned face, wide cheek-bones; his head that was too large for his narrow shoulders; his dark woolly-springy hair trimmed close to his skull; his skin that was earth-colored, rich and smooth with something smoldering coppery-red inside it; skin that would be hot to the touch, unlike my winter-chapped skin that was cold to the touch as if the pale flesh were numb, without sensation. The fact that Vernor Matheius was "Negro" did not seem to me more remarkable than any other of his qualities; these qualities were remarkable because they were Vernor Matheius's and because (as it seemed to me) he had chosen them.

For here was the paradox: in philosophy, one is trained to distinguish between the *essential* and the *accidental*; in our own personalities, there is said to be that which is *essential*, and that which is *accidental*; yet such was Vernor Matheius's uniqueness in my eyes, there could be nothing *accidental* about him. If he was Negro, it must be that he'd chosen to be so; he had chosen Negro-ness; Negro-ness had not chosen him. And so I did not isolate the man's Negro-ness from any other quality of his (of those qualities of which I was aware, for I felt about Vernor Matheius as I'd felt one day opening a copy of Wittgenstein's *Tractatus Logico-Philosophicus* in a secondhand bookstore, riddled with underlinings and annotations in faded ink: here was mystery, here was an intelligence I could not measure). It was a fact of his being but not a definitive fact.

That morning when the professor called upon Vernor Matheius to speak, a heated exchange suddenly developed; the subject was a precise definition of "idealism"—which, in philosophical terms, is much different from ordinary usage; Vernor Matheius made a shrewd, sarcastic comment, and laughter rippled through the lecture hall, and the professor recoiled, annoyed, his authority challenged, and spoke curtly and coldly to Vernor Matheius; as an indulgent father at last speaks to a favored son, revealing that, perhaps, the favored son is not so favored after all. The rest of us, looking on, were startled and thrilled—even I who loved Vernor Matheius was thrilled. The professor's condemnatory words were, "Mr. Matheius," with an ironic

inflection on the second syllable, drawing out the "ei," "—your soph-
istry ceases to amuse."

I saw the hurt and the humiliation in Vernor Matheius's face,
which was creased, almost wizened like a squeezed-together leather
glove; his eyes appeared moist as quickly he lowered his chin, his
mouth tightening like a knot. There was a moment's pained silence;
then politely and almost inaudibly Vernor Matheius murmured an
apology. I thought *He has been wounded to the heart. He, too!*

It was as if I'd had a hand in that wounding.

STANDING THEN IN the aisle beside Vernor Matheius's row, as he
made his way in my direction, not seeing me at first; meaning to
offer words of sympathy, commiseration. What a roaring in my ears!
How the hardwood floor tilted, like a drunken ship! Of course I
could not speak his name—"Vernor." For a terrible moment I could
not speak at all. The man's physical presence confused me, his height,
he was at least a head taller than I, towering over me; a powerful
throbbing heat lifted from him, as if he were sweating inside his
clothes; his skin dark and smoldering with blood; close up, his skin
was darker and coarser than I'd imagined. Behind the smudged lenses
of his wire-rimmed glasses his eyes were damp and glaring. He wore
a white shirt and even a necktie, both rumpled, not-clean; with an
air of sullen dignity he was shrugging into the bulky sheepskin jacket
and with rapid deft motions winding the crimson wool scarf around
his neck; as if, in his fury, he would have liked to strangle himself;
his fingers remarkably long, his hands rather narrow, the palms curiously pinkish-pale as if they might be soft, even tender to the touch.
I saw that he wanted only to escape the lecture hall, the last thing
he wanted was to speak with anyone who had witnessed his public
humiliation, yet I followed beside him as he pushed into the aisle, I
stammered words meant to console; to my astonishment I saw my
hand reach out timidly to touch his—*his* hand; but at the last second

I dared touch only the soiled cuff of his jacket; if I'd touched his skin he might have flung my hand off in sheer nervous reaction; and all the while I was smiling, trying to smile, a fixed ghastly grin, in longing and terror seeking the very source of terror for solace, protection. *I can love you, I am the one who can love you. Who am I except the one whose sole identity is that she can love you?*

Vernor Matheius was staring at me. It was as if he'd heard, not my shy halting insipid speech, not my well-intentioned words in imitation of such gestures of commiseration made to me by women or girls who'd hoped to console me for whatever hurts, deprivations, but my desperate thoughts. *I, I can love you!* He had seen, not felt, the brush of my fingers against his sleeve; how near I'd come to touching him. Sharply he said, "Yes? What?"—still staring at me, as if I'd accosted him; yet at the same time he was turning on his heel to escape; rudely giving me no time to answer, had I had an answer; he bounded up the steps to the rear exit, and was gone.

Yet: I have done it, touched you. And now you know me.

TO WIN VERNOR MATHEIUS'S attention, I understood that I would have to make myself visible to him, and "attractive"; I would have to reinvent myself; I shopped for secondhand clothing in the city, choosing things I myself would never have wished to wear, or dared: a lime-green suede jacket in a bygone style, only slightly worn at the cuffs and elbows; a ruffled red long-sleeved silk blouse that looked like an explosion on my narrow torso; a tartan plaid wool skirt several sizes too large for me made of an exquisitely beautiful fabric; a sleek-sexy black linen dress with a V-neck and a dropped hemline and an unraveling hem. Out of bins marked $3–$5 I pulled a sweater, a gauzy scarf, a belt made of linked silver ornaments. Each of the items had been many times reduced—the suede jacket, for instance, had been marked down from $95 to $43 to $19—and was certainly a bargain; these were quality clothes of the kind I could never have afforded new; but I could not really afford even these bargains, and had had to borrow money from girls in my residence, even as I suspected I would never be able to repay it—I'd become reckless, shameless. And my hair that fell now to my shoulders in an untidy rippled-curly mass needed attention: trimming, shaping, "styling": I found myself one Saturday morning in a neighborhood beauty salon spending $12 on my hair; staring amazed at the transformed girl in the mirror as the beautician (a heavily made-up, glamorous woman of approximately the age my mother would have been had she lived) said cheerfully, "Some improvement, eh?"

9

In the gloomy coffee house Vernor Matheius talked of philosophy almost exclusively. Passionately, his eyes shining; his voice low, intimate, gravelly-musical. *As if we were a couple, we two. As if we were lovers.* He was known here, when we'd stepped inside several people called out "Hello, Vernor!" to him; near the front, in a window alcove, an elderly white-haired man and an intense boy I recognized from my German class were playing chess on a chess board inlaid in a small table; both glanced up and smiled distractedly at Vernor, and seemed not to see me at all. We sat in a rear, darkly lit booth with a sticky table top; Vernor zestfully ordered coffee for us both; strong black bitter-almond coffee of a kind I had never tasted before; the caffeine swiftly coursed through my veins, my pulse quickened, my very eyeballs began to throb. *As if lovers. We two.* After asking my name and quizzing me briefly about philosophy—strange to him, that "a girl like you" would be drawn to philosophy, so few "girls" were—he spoke of Aristotle, Descartes, Leipnitz, Spinoza, Wittgenstein, and Cassirier; "the universal laws of structure and operation"—the only truly worthy concern of mankind. When he'd first gone to college he had believed he might be a teacher, but he'd discovered how empty, how ignorant, how deadly education courses were; he'd spent a year in a seminary hoping to learn of God but discovered only a human, confused, and contradictory God—"a Yahweh like a collective nightmare of mankind." Above all, he couldn't tolerate history for what is history but a mass of accidents, most of them bloody; a record of man's cruelty; cruelty compounded by ignorance; mankind like ants of different races, creeds, languages battling one another for dominance; for mere anthills; what is politics but raging self-interest and aggression; even the current civil rights movement—he uttered "civil rights movement" with a respectful, neutral detachment as if it were a foreign phrase—was a distraction from the purity of the philosophical quest: to know what *is*. "Every year is the same year, every moment is the same moment! The only truths that matter are the truths that transcend time." How emphatic Vernor Matheius's voice, how hypnotic. How his large handsome head, his animated dark-tinctured face loomed above me, his eyes showing pale crescents of white above the rim of the iris. He gave off a warm, bodily odor that mixed with the sharp smell of the coffee and rushed along my veins swelling my veins making me perspire inside my clothes. I could not interrupt him to explain that I had to leave for my residence hall, I was scheduled to work in the cafeteria at five; for suddenly it was five, and after five; and too late.

I can leave him, I can turn away at any time. For now Vernor Matheius was leading me along the wide windy twilit avenue; now he was closer beside me, his fingers gripping my green suede jacket at the elbow; we came to Chambers Street and descended the icy sidewalk; *I am free to turn away to run away at any time* though if I drifted from him his fingers gripped my elbow tighter. And there was the stucco apartment building at 1183 Chambers, how suddenly this place I should not have recognized; I was smiling a fixed, forced smile; I believed that I had chosen this; though I did not know what exactly I had chosen. *Free to leave, to turn away. To run.* As we were climbing the stairway; the stairway I should not have known of, and seemed not to know of; the stairway of my dreams that was a crude wood-plank outdoor stairway with a roof but otherwise open to weather, the steps beginning to rot, swaying slightly beneath us. Vernor Matheius was close behind me, I was just ahead of him; I thought *He is herding me the way a dog herds sheep* and the thought made me laugh. Vernor was joking nervously about his "living quarters"—he was "an underground man aboveground"—there was the surprise of his icy-cold fingers encircling my right leg just below the knee; they were quick, strong, deft fingers; I tried to shake them off as if this was a game; of course it was a game; we behaved as if it was a game, playful and laughing; I thought *He would not hurt me—would he?* There was a garbagey smell, a smell of rotting wood. I opened my mouth to speak yet could not, the words tangled together. I had to leave, I was late for my job in the cafeteria, I had no money, I was desperately poor and would never be able to repay the girls to whom I owed money, a total of $87.50, a sum that might as well have been $10,000. I could not say these things; I could not say that I loved him but was terrified of him; that I had never been with a man or a boy like this; I was terrified of becoming pregnant; "becoming pregnant" was a thought that terrified me though I had no sexual experience; I could not exert any will contrary to Vernor Matheius's will, the playful grip of his fingers at my knee; as in a dream we are unable to exert any will contrary to the inscrutable will of the dream. It might have been (I thought) that whatever was to happen had already happened; in philosophy there was the theoretical possibility of the isomorphic universe, symmetrical in both space and time; a strictly determined universe that could run forward and backward; to exert will in such a universe was not possible; to be blamed would be unjust. And so now I was climbing the outdoor stairway at 1183 Chambers Street exactly as I'd wished in my dreams; and yet this was not at all the dream I'd wished; I was frightened, and felt sick; I was trembling badly, as if freezing; the bitter black coffee of which I'd had only two or three sips now rose acid and bilious in my throat. *It's the green suede jacket that has brought me here!* I was thinking. *It's the smiling-lipsticked girl in the mirror* I was thinking. Biting my lip to keep from laughing, thinking *This is what a pretty girl does, it's time you knew. This is what a "desired" girl does, this is what is done to a "desired" girl.*

Vernor Matheius fumbled with the key trying quickly to open the door to apartment 2D before we were seen, and pushed me inside. For once wordless.

MORTAL LOVE

BRIAN HALL

 MADELEINE, TWO AND a half years old, was in the bathtub, telling my wife Pamela a story:

She (Madeleine) went to Stewart Park and swam. Then she went to Taughannock Park and swam. She didn't sink ("go blblblbl") because something was helping her float. Then she got out of the water, and a bug helped her dry off. Then she went to Old MacDonald's, and there was a pool there, too. So she was in the pool. It wasn't very deep. She was eating oranges. The juice was getting in the water, but the juice didn't mind. The oranges would have minded, but they weren't getting in the water.

Madeleine loved her baths, but with an undercurrent of anxiety. Her toys had to be out before the plug was pulled, because otherwise the drain would swallow them. In *Madeline's Rescue*, the eponymous heroine had gone blblblbl in the river Seine. In another book we had been reading lately, *The Sorcerer's Apprentice*, water rose out of a tub and almost drowned everybody, so Madeleine now whimpered and pleaded with us to stop when we added more hot water: "I'm worried about it overflowing!" In her own story, she had to assure herself (via Pamela) that she wasn't sinking, that the pool at MacDonald's wasn't deep, that the oranges were safely out of the water.

Why oranges? She had been eating them that evening. Why a bug? That was less obvious, and more interesting. "Something" had kept Madeleine afloat, and in the next instant she thought of the bug, and the bug helped her dry off. The bug was saving her, from the water, from sinking, from—well, what? What was the word?

She knew the word, but not from any of her books. In *Will's New Cap*, Will fell down, and in *The Goat and her Kids*, the wolf was butted into the water, and in *Asleep Asleep*, a variety of animals snoozed, and in *Everyone Poops*, everyone pooped. But no one died.

She knew the word, in fact, from bugs. They lay in the window casements and in corners, not moving, dried to husks. She used to say that the flies on the flypaper were sleeping, but that was back at the very beginning of her speech, and who knew what she had meant by "sleeping"? Now she knew that sleeping things woke up, and the bugs on their backs in the corners did not. She knew they did not, because we assured her they did not, as we showed her the body of a yellow jacket or a roll-up bug, and asked her if she wanted to hold it, and she worried it might spring to life in her hand. It can't, hon, we said. It's dead.

Dead.

She would hold the dead thing in the palm of her hand. It was "little tiny," too. The bugs inspired affection and awe. She wanted to help them, but they were beyond her, beyond everything. They knew something she didn't know. They couldn't be hurt, we said, when we vacuumed them up. In a way, they were safe. So instead, the bug in the bathtub story helped Madeleine. From its position of safety and knowledge, it knew how to save her. In a way, it was her guardian spirit. After all, Pamela called Madeleine "Love Bug."

Insect companions began to appear in other stories. She told me one day she was a soldier from China: "I came by car. First I went to China and stayed for five minutes, then I came back, and then I went to the North Pole and came back."

"You went all that way by car?" I said, impressed.

"Yes! I was holding a bumblebee in one hand."

While Pamela one evening cut my hair, Madeleine hacked away with a dull pair of scissors at Big Baby's glistening polymeric strands. There were bumblebees in Big Baby's hair, she informed us, "but they're dead, so they don't mind getting stepped on."

Love, death, bugs. In *A Best Friend for Frances*, Frances's little sister Gloria said, in my best pathetic voice, "I wish I had a friend."

"Is she sad?" Madeleine asked, perturbed.

She had apparently mulled this over, seeking a solution. She came up to me one afternoon and brightly demanded, "Daddy, say, 'I wish I had a friend.'"

"I wish I had a friend."

Madeleine hopped, brimming over. "I'll give you a friend! I'll give you a ladybug! It can't crawl away, because it's dead! It's a *real* dead ladybug!"

In fact, it was a pretend dead ladybug. Madeleine led me to the place on the wall of her room where its tiny invisible corpse was stuck. Gently removing it, she placed it in my palm.

I sobbed in gratitude. A friend!

But our relationship with these mortal familiars was more complicated. Spring came. Whenever I found a spider in the house, I caught it in a glass and Madeleine, following me outside, would ask, as I pitched it into the grass, "Does the spider like that?" and I would say, "Yes, her food is outside." I didn't save flies, however. I swatted them. Moreover, Madeleine helped me. She pointed them out, or ran after them herself, ineffectually waving the swatter and giggling. When they woke her, like us, early in the morning, she would urge, "Whack it, Daddy," while I traipsed up and down the bed in my underwear. But when, yelping in triumph, I did finally whack it, she would venture, "The fly doesn't like that?" and I would reply, picking it piecemeal off the swatter netting, "No, honey, the fly doesn't like that."

Her giggle, when she chased the fly, showed her ambivalence. "Don't hit" was one of the fundamental rules, but I hit them, so it must be all right. And yet, they didn't like it. I was putting them beyond hurting, but it certainly looked like I was hurting them.

She had to work on this. That spring, Kaia, the white cat at her friend Theodore's house, disappeared. It went into the woods and never came back, like a toy going down the drain.

"Did Kaia die?" Madeleine asked.

"We don't know," I said. "Maybe."

"Maybe she's living with someone else."

"Maybe."

Madeleine vaguely knew now that first you grew up, and then you got old. Grandpas Al and Larry had white hair because they were old. Grandpa Al walked with a cane because his body didn't work so well anymore.

"Do people die?" she asked.

"Yes."

"Will you and Mama die?"

Well. There it was. She had zeroed in on it faster than I had expected. "Everybody eventually dies," I said, reflexively holding off the D-word with the arm-long "eventually."

"You and Mama, too?"

"Ye-es. But that would be a long time from now. Very long."

"How long?"

"Longer than you can imagine."

That, of course, was part of the problem. She *couldn't* imagine. The milestones of her future now read: Birth of Conor or Cora, Daddy's Birthday, Madeleine's Birthday, Christmas, Death of Parents.

"Many years away," I said.

She reached as high as she could. "By the time you're twenty?"

"I'm already older than twenty."

This seemed only to alarm her. How old was I, anyway?

I said, "You will be all grown up and you'll have kids before I die. Even when you have kids, I'll still live for many years, many times longer than your whole life so far. Believe me, it's a long long time away. Way way far away."

Thus, for the first time, did I deliberately lie to her, promising certainty where of course there was none.

I wondered how she pictured our deaths. Would we just stop moving, like the bugs? But the bugs had not inspired her to ask about our own deaths, whereas the disappearance of Kaia had. She had feared, from before she knew what fear was, that we might go away and not come back.

One night when we were ending a visit to some friends, Madeleine turned to their nine-year-old daughter and, perhaps on the subject of leave-taking, said to her in a matter-of-fact tone, "You're ebenchewie going to die."

"What?" the girl asked.

"Eventually," I clarified. "Dead. You."

Throughout that spring and summer, every few days Madeleine would ask me out of the blue, "Who died?"

"Eleanor Roosevelt, she's dead," I usually said.

"Who else?" She wore a cautious smile. This was the way to deal with the subject, to turn it into a game, or try to.

"Winston Churchill is dead, too."

"Who else?"

After three or four more names, I often drew a blank for a moment. Like Madeleine when asked to imagine a food for her dolls, I was flooded by my choices, and my synapses shorted. "Oh, yes," I'd finally say. "Plato. He died a *long* time ago."

*   *   *

A FEW WEEKS later, Madeleine became a big sister.

Pamela's and my propaganda blitz had been three-pronged. *Big Like Me* presented the older sibling as wise mentor, lucky to have a disciple: "Hello Baby, little tiny baby. This is me. I'm going to show you everything." *A Baby Just Like Me* hammered away at the need for patience, as the big sister wondered, month after month, when this useless bundle demanding all her parents' attention would turn into a playmate. *Mommy and Daddy and I Are Having a Baby* had assigned itself a more modest task: to prepare the kid for the sight of her mother in pain, yowling, spouting blood, and pushing out a misshapen, glistening creature of uncertain species.

The books probably prepared Madeleine for sisterhood about as well as my pinching Pamela's arm in our birth class had prepared her for her first labor. I always emphasized, as we read them, that the time covered in the first two books was more than a year, which put that future sibling-as-playmate off somewhere between next Christmas and my death. And as for the third book, Madeleine always asked us to skip the drawing that showed the mother's face in a grimace, the blood pooling out from the place where the gorgon's head sprouted like a purple cabbage.

Pamela's labor began at around 4:00 A.M. and by 7:00 the two midwives were at the house. Knowing that cows, or at least the idea of them, had long been familiar to Madeleine, we told her that Mama would be mooing, and she seemed less upset than intrigued by the long low moans. As Pamela rocked, Madeleine occasionally sat near her and made a histrionic gesture of stroking her foot sympathetically. As one would expect at this age, the action seemed less a real offering of solace than an expression of Madeleine's need, at this disturbing moment, to be noticed and appreciated for her grown-up solicitude.

My parents had come from Boston a few days previously to help out, and when the midwives suggested some exercise to urge the labor onward, Pamela and I proposed to Madeleine that she stay with

Grandma Peggy and Grandpa Al at the sandbox while we went for a walk. "Sure!" she said brightly, running to Grandma Peggy, while we turned toward the road, saying to each other, "So mature! So independent!" As we reached the end of the driveway we heard a cry, and here came Madeleine, bawling, running with that endearing toddler hop, back on her heels, her arms bouncing with the effort of maintaining speed. We decided to cut the husband-and-wife-as-a-team crap and have Pamela walk with one of the midwives, while I stayed back with Madeleine. Pamela would be able to focus better on the labor if she was sure Madeleine was happy, and the sandbox was pretty new and enthralling, so we patted and dug and made sand cones while Pamela walked two miles.

By noon we were all back in the house, and it was time to push. Grandma Peggy, as planned, unveiled a big new floor puzzle for Madeleine in the playroom while Pamela kneeled by the living room couch with her elbows in my lap. Pamela gave a couple of trial grunts, at the sound of which Madeleine promptly appeared, twirling her hair and chomping on her pacifier with that deadpan heavy-lidded expression I recognized as fright. I smiled at her over Pamela's head but she didn't see me. With a loud grinding shout, Pamela gave the first big push, and either the shout or the sight of the baby's head popping into view—that page she had never wanted to see—was too much, and Madeleine turned and ran back into the playroom. I expected to hear a siren wail come sailing out, but instead she returned with her grandmother in tow, just in time for the second shout and push. My mother gestured to me a question about leading Madeleine away, but the baby was already born, having shot out so fast that the midwives had been caught by surprise and were now jointly grappling with the greasy body and struggling to shake open towels. Madeleine's fright seemed to be giving way to a glimmer of interest.

In the confusion, one of the midwives had mistaken the other's pinky for a penis, and for thirty seconds Madeleine had a little brother. But by the time the baby latched onto the breast we knew it was a girl. She sucked avidly and Pamela laughed and the midwives hymned midwiferal praise. I took Madeleine on my lap and we sat in the penumbra, leaning toward the spotlight. Subdued, Madeleine stared. Useless bundle, cynosure, tiny baby, animate doll, pink stork-bitten sucker, future playmate, little sister, interloper, rival. It all had a name now: Cora.

MADELEINE, STANDING ON the toy chest, supervised diaper changes. She would undo the Velcro on the diaper cover and shout the news, to whichever parent was absent, regarding the amount, color, and consistency of Cora's poop. She wanted to hold Cora in her lap on the couch, and we took pictures, praising her big-sisterly gentleness. In those first photos, Madeleine is smiling for the camera, but her eyes have a haunted cast. What has happened? she seems to be thinking. What now?

"Mama!" she would announce toward the end of Cora's nap, striding importantly into the room, "Cora is going, 'Aanh!'" She would throw open the bathroom door and pull aside the shower curtain to inform a rapidly cooling Pamela, "Just so you know— Cora's looking for the breast." She assumed Cora wanted a pacifier, and kept trying to plug one in her mouth until a cup of sour milk shot out and she leaped back, asking, "What happened?" People came by and wisely brought presents for both girls, telling Madeleine what a good big sister she was, and how lucky, and wasn't she happy?

"Yes," Madeleine said, smiling.

She hugged Cora in the mornings, beaming down on her. Sometimes she hugged too hard. She wanted to carry Cora around like a doll, and our argument that she might drop her little sister didn't seem to impress her as a significant objection. She bounced a red field ball in the room where Cora was sleeping, and wouldn't stop until we took it away. She jiggled Cora gently in her cloth bouncy seat, garnering praise, and every now and then pulled the frame down so hard before releasing it that perhaps I wasn't the only one to imagine the seat acting like a catapult and tossing Cora out the nearest window. She clapped her hands in Cora's face, making her cry, and when we asked her why she was doing it, she smiled and said, "Because I want to!"

Those smiles were all the same. Appeasement gestures ("Take this cup away from me") rather than signals of pleasure, they were wide and almost flat, only a hair's breadth away from the grimace that precedes crying. Before I had children of my own, I had occasionally witnessed parents gently reasoning with some obnoxious brat and had inwardly seethed, "What that kid really needs is. . . ." Now I saw it differently. Madeleine had lost her place as the sole center of the universe. When I saw her harass Cora, I moved to protect the baby, but felt in myself a warm surge of love and sympathy for the aggressor. She needed us. She needed reassurance. The cool observer in me, the clinician, was impressed by the easy power of parental love.

Pamela and I had arranged our work so that she had no commitments for several months, and I none for six weeks. We had agreed ahead of time that I would mainly take care of Cora, so that Madeleine could receive as much attention and reassurance as possible from her mother, whom she had most feared losing, and to whom she had presciently clung so fiercely during the pregnancy that I had jokingly started referring to myself as "chopped liver."

By the end of the first month Madeleine had noticed that Cora, except when she wanted to nurse, didn't seem to prefer Pamela to me. "Cora doesn't call you chopped liver," was how she put it. It took her a day or two to mull over this, after which, on the occasion of a request for me to help her do some leaf rubbings, she made my rehabilitation official: "You're not chopped liver any more, Daddy." I mock-sobbed that I would try to savor this fleeting moment of favor. But of course I was pleased, and not just for myself. Now Madeleine's mixed feelings could be spread between both parents, making it easier for all of us to handle. The interloper liked me, so I couldn't be all bad, so my attention was a better comforter when Cora stole Pamela away for nursing.

During Pamela's pregnancy, Madeleine had increasingly assumed the role of big sister or parent in her play with her dolls. She had had me construct a cardboard cradle to match the one we had borrowed for the coming baby, and she rocked her favorite doll, Hans, in it, occasionally bringing him a bedtime bottle of water and explaining to me, "Hans is saying, 'I want juice!' but I'm saying, 'No, you can only have water, because you've already brushed your teeth.'" She was, as usual, being so obedient that her wishes and ours were virtually indistinguishable. Through the books we had read with her we had signaled our desire that she act like a big sister, and she was acting up a storm.

However, as soon as Cora was born, Madeleine's interest in Hans, and all her dolls, declined precipitously. The role of big sister had become too pressing, too charged with ambivalent feelings, to be an attractive game. In real life she soldiered on, instinctive obedience struggling with rational rebelliousness. She had me commemorate her vigilance over the diaper changing in a series of drawings. I've kept one which shows Cora on the changing pad, I engrossed in her rear end, and Madeleine supervising from the toy chest, smiling benignly and saying (so accepting! so generous!) "I want to hold the baby." But I also remember that Madeleine, even as she continued to insist on witnessing the unveiling of the poop, developed the habit of gagging down into it. It was ritualized, but it was from the heart. She was gagging at the shit, which was becoming more solid, and smellier, but also, I think, at the sight of Cora, at the whole thought of her, and at the thought of her own big sisterhood. Next to the picture

I've saved of Cora getting her diaper changed is another that Madeleine demanded: *Madeleine* getting her diaper changed.

That was the core of it, wasn't it? All of Madeleine's ambivalence about growing up had rushed back at the sight of this little creature who so completely and inarguably needed us, who still lived in wholeness, before any awareness of the difference between Cora and not-Cora, before knowledge and responsibility and disobedience and time. Pamela and I were infallible gods in our relationship with Cora, it was no illusion, we were the breast and the hands to carry her there, we were everything she needed, right on the premises, walking in the garden. Shut outside, looking in, Madeleine felt the yearning at the core of the world's religions: the desire to be a child in the hands of an all-powerful god, a brainless sheep protected by its shepherd, a drop dissolved into the oversoul. Freud called it *thanatos*, the death instinct, but I think a less highfalutin Greek word is more apposite: nostalgia. Madeleine ached to return home, where she would fit so well into not-Madeleine you wouldn't be able to see the cracks.

Madeleine sat on a towel, placed a cork or a pacifier at her crotch, pulled the front of the towel up to her stomach and commanded, "Say: 'Did you poop in your diapers?' " Pooping was the ongoing, unignorable process of separating not-Madeleine from Madeleine. By hoarding it in the diaper one retained an ersatz wholeness. At night she wanted to wear a real diaper, and our reminders of how proud she had been, just four months ago, to sleep without one were to no avail. She told us she would poop in the diaper, and we blanched and cajoled and appealed to some vestige of pride in her age, and she assured us she would only pretend to poop. A day or two later she said she wanted to really do it, and we said, No, pretend, and she said, No, really, and we said, No, pretend, and she said, What she had meant all along was, she would pretend to really do it, and we said, Fine. We discussed it again the next night, and the next, and the string of reallys was getting longer, the admission of pretence more uncertain. Please, we were saying, with what must have been pleasingly frank fear, please don't. Please don't.

She didn't. But her price was a long wallow in coprocentric daydreams and playacting. Her favorite reenactment, for weeks and weeks, was of a scene that had been common during the previous winter: we at the house of friends, and she with shit in her diaper. She would be in costume, with the diaper on. She wanted the game strung out in excruciating detail, beginning with my speech about the fact that we had to go soon, and she had *ten minutes* more, and after ten minutes she would have to get her diaper changed. "Why?" she would ask, and the first time we had played she had fed me my answer, word for word: "Because you'll fall asleep in the car and get a rash."

Did she promise?

"I promise!" she would say, and play at playing for a few seconds. Then: "Say, 'You have *five minutes!*'"

I had to go through three minutes and one minute, and she kept promising, and ultimately of course refused. "Then what did you do?" she breathed.

"We held you down."

"Did I like that?"

"No, you didn't."

"What did I say?"

"You cried."

She would want me to really hold her down.

And would she really cry? I asked.

No.

But it was close.

"I didn't like this the first time around," I complained.

But I submitted, because the game so clearly served needs beyond her mania, reminding her of a blessed time before Cora and displacing the conflict she felt *now* about wanting to shit in her diaper and us not wanting her to.

One night Madeleine was lying on the living room floor, tired, having had no nap that day, and Pamela was holding Cora in her arms and singing "I Wonder As I Wander." By the end of the song, Cora was asleep, and Pamela and I sat quietly for a minute, contemplating our two beautiful daughters, the quiet evening, the startling passage of time. We sang the song again, together, to Madeleine, and at the end asked, "Do you remember when we used to sing that for you?" Madeleine twirled her hair and said nothing.

We began "I Gave My Love a Cherry," but stopped.

"Are you a little bit sad?" I asked. (This was the phrase she herself used, when upset: "I'm alittlebitsad.") She clearly was, but she shook her head and turned over, pushed my hand away, sucked on her pacifier and twirled on, her eyes distant and half-closed.

"Why are you sad, honey?" Pamela asked.

"I don't know," she quavered.

Pamela and I traded a glance. We had not forgotten her dislike of lullabies, back when she had slept in the hated crib and knew that songs meant we wanted her to get into it. But that arrangement had ended six months ago. Bedding down now with us, she fell asleep to the sound of reading. She had heard so little singing in the past half year that her sense of pitch had slipped dramatically. And anyway, our singing to Cora didn't seem to bother her.

Pamela tried to put Cora down, but she woke up, so I held her and sang another song until she fell asleep again. Now I was in the armchair, with Cora asleep on my shoulder, and Pamela and Madeleine were on the couch looking at a book of poems. One of them was "Hush, Little Baby," and Pamela, endeavoring to figure out where we stood, started singing it. She got about two lines in before Madeleine fell apart.

"Why?" she howled, tears spilling. "Why?" It was a voice of

such bleak pain and confusion that I felt tears crowding into my own eyes.

"Do you mean why does it make you sad?" Pamela asked.

"Yes."

"I don't know, honey. Do you know?"

"No."

The next day, I asked Madeleine if she remembered sleeping in the crib, and she said Yes. "What do you remember?"

"I called 'Mama' and 'Daddy.' I stuck my legs out."

That was true. She used to put her legs through the bars as a game and a delaying tactic. "Did you not like sleeping in the crib?"

"No."

"Why not?"

"I was afraid you'd go away."

"Go away?"

"I was afraid you'd get in the car and go away somewhere and leave me alone."

Since she had been much less articulate when she was in the crib, this was the first I'd heard of it. I wondered if it came from *Carl's Masquerade*, in which the parents went off to a party, leaving the baby in her crib for the dog to watch over. Or perhaps it was a reasonable extrapolation from our sneaking out of the room.

"Is that why you don't like us to sing, because it reminds you of when you slept in the crib?"

Madeleine pulled out her pacifier and glanced away from me, squinting. This was the expression she used when she was about to say something she considered mature (and it was interesting how much the flourish of the pacifier-removal looked like similar adult flourishes with pipes or glasses, before similarly self-important pro-nouncements). "I don't think so," she said.

Neither did I. Perhaps memory of the crib was part of it, but her attitude toward lullabies back then had been impatient and resistant, not sad.

Music, like odors, can unlock not just memories but buried moods, whole past states of being. Pamela and I had sung lullabies to Madeleine every day of her life and then had stopped—when?— oh, long ago, it must have seemed to her, back when she was what she termed "a little tiny baby." But last night she had been lying down, twirling her hair, and suddenly we were standing over her again and singing one of those old songs, and she had been transported back. It hardly mattered whether her associations of that past existence were good (pre-Cora) or bad (crib), whether she felt nostalgia or trauma, or a stew of both. Simply, it was *past*, and it is painful to feel, deep and sharp in your body, the passing of time, the irrecoverability of the past, the death of your past self (now briefly, bruisingly haunting you), and, by implication, the future death of your present self, the treacherous changing and slipping away of bugs and parents and all things.

The Why? that Madeleine had demanded of an unanswering world the night before had affected me so strongly because it sounded so bereft, so—I would have said—adult. But the word I had been groping for was, perhaps, *human*. In front of my eyes, Madeleine, poignantly, was shedding present-tense toddlerhood and becoming a person: ducked in the river, swept onward, clutching reeds that had failed to hold her.

ON LOVING CHARACTERS

ANGELA DAVIS-GARDNER

for Larry

THE FIRST FICTIONAL characters I loved were those in other people's books. Heidi, the Five Little Peppers, and especially Jo, writing her plays, were my friends. Later I was, with Scarlett, torn between Ashley and Rhett. I didn't in the usual sense love Dostoevsky's Raskalnikov or Tolstoy's Ivan Ilych or Flaubert's Madame Bovary (deeply flawed characters all), but I had for them the kind of understanding and sympathy in which love is grounded.

In the voracious reading of my twenties I was unconsciously searching for what Wallace Stevens called in the title of one poem "How to Live. What to Do." I began reading Walker Percy's *The Last Gentleman* during the first week or so of a job I'd landed in public relations. It was, on the surface, a fine job on a lovely college campus working with congenial people. The salary and benefits were good; I had a secretary, and a large, pleasant office. But the work, fund raising and putting out an alumni magazine, seemed to have nothing to do with me. I was much more like Percy's Will Barrett, "a watcher and a listener and a wanderer" whose problem was "ruling out the possible." Will was doing something about his problem, setting up a telescope in a New York meadow, spying, figuring out the geometry of his emotions; I was only reading about it during my lunch breaks. One day with Will's subtle, intelligent voice in my head, I walked into my boss's office and said I was sorry, I had to resign, I'd made a mistake. It was an uncomfortable scene; I was embarrassed, I had no good excuse. But I walked out exhilarated. I was like Will, full of the possible; life was too important to be lived out in boredom.

Actually figuring out what to do took a lot longer, ten years or so at various jobs, all of them performed more responsibly than the first one, but none of them fulfilling either. The possibility of writing was always there like a shadow I didn't want to look behind myself to see. My teachers had thought I'd be a writer, and my family too, but I had some doubts, mixed in with a good dollop of rebelliousness. It was finally a trio of characters—my own this time—who beguiled me into writing fiction.

I was in my thirties, married, no children (though I wanted children); my editing job was not only mind-numbing but tainted by office politics. My husband kindly suggested I take some time off work. The first day of freedom I bought a black-and-white speckled notebook, the kind of composition book I'd used in school. During walks in the woods near our house, I began writing down what I saw. Soon I was writing down other things, too: images, dreams, ideas for stories.

One of the story ideas had its origin in my past, in the history of my favorite grandmother, for whom I'd been named and who had seen gifts in me—an aptitude for piano, for one—that my parents did not seem to recognize. This grandmother had been born into a French Acadian family in Nova Scotia, but her parents drowned at sea when she was a young girl and she was placed in a convent school to be raised by nuns. Though she had died when I was in high school before telling me anything about her childhood, I'd been fascinated all my life by the few snippets of information my mother was able to provide: the Bay of Fundy tides that sucked out forty feet, stranding lobsters which the students gathered for convent meals; the requirement that the girls bathe in their underwear; a legendary shipwreck survivor—an armless, legless foreigner, apparently mute—who spent his entire life in a village near the convent without ever revealing his tragic story.

What if, I wrote one day, a young, orphaned girl at a convent on the Bay of Fundy found a tongueless man, a shipwreck survivor, washed up on the shore, and he were brought back to the convent to be nursed back to life? I was drawn to creating a life for this young girl—first named Maria, then Felice—because I wanted to try to understand what my grandmother had lived through, and how that might have affected my mother and then me, that experience of loss handed down through the generations.

But after the gestation of the novel, which began with a cluster of images—the convent kitchen, the nuns' bowls and black shoes, sand breasts built on the beach by repressed young girls reaching puberty in an atmosphere of repression—the character and her world began to exist on their own. Soon Felice was Felice, and not my grandmother. Felice had a mentor, an elderly, nearly blind nun, Sister Agatha, who also sprang from a handful of particular details: black plates on a white cloth so she could see to eat; Masaccio's painting (which I'd recently seen in Italy) of Adam and Eve being expelled from the garden; a painting on a convent wall (I had this image from a friend) of the martyrdom of Saint Agatha, her lopped-off breasts being carried away on a huge platter by Roman soldiers. Sister Agatha was fond of quoting Gerard Manley Hopkins, a Jesuit poet who suffered his creativity like a scourge; the nun herself, before blindness and age set in, had been a painter who gloried in the sensuality of the physical world. Soon Felice and Sister Agatha were talking and acting on their own. Sister Agatha, improvising from Hopkins and his "long live the weeds and the wilderness yet," began mumbling about the fine qualities of weeds, their tenacity and unappreciated beauty; in the stern environment of the convent, she encouraged Felice toward weediness. Felice led the other girls on bold midnight forays to peek inside the room where the tongueless man lay. And Felice—with Sister Agatha's prodding—became a pianist, with aspirations of composing, in spite of the fact I knew nothing about music beyond the lessons my grandmother had given me.

My feelings about these characters, and to some degree all my characters since, is something akin to maternal love. But this is especially true of Felice. Before I had a child she was the one I didn't think I'd have. When she finally, after much travail, went off to Random House, I felt the kind of wistfulness a mother has watching her child leave home; she'd never be known to me again in the same full intimate way.

The writer Harumi Murakami said that for him writing a novel is like falling in love. "I don't have love affairs," he said, "because I write novels." The love affair he's talking about, I believe, is the absorption in creating the world of the novel and all its characters. The novel demands the writer's most passionate committment to the characters he or she is imagining into life. Characters in short stories also require the writer's loving attention, but, unless the same characters reappear in many stories, these are usually less intense relationships.

Characters, in my experience, are created from the inside out. Our first impressions of people in the actual world are visual and aural. In our real life relationships we are prejudiced, perhaps forever, by our senses. With my characters, on the other hand, although I may know a few salient details of appearance, it's really the motivation, the problems, the history and the actions that I'm engaged with in the process of creation. Full physical appearance of the character is often the last thing that comes to me. The way this usually happens is that I see someone in the "real" world who *is* that character. I'd almost finished writing about Felice when I saw a girl I was convinced was her, working in a camera shop in Chapel Hill. I went back often to buy film, trying to be inconspicuous, not to stare. The main character in my second novel, a girl named Beryl, I had a briefer glimpse of on an airport escalator, but I was equally thrilled. It was as though she, like Felice, really existed. Beryl's father had not quite jelled in my mind until I saw a man rocking his baby one day in a pediatrician's office where I had taken my sick child. He was a short man with an acne-scarred face and the tenderest expression as he looked down at his child; it was the kind of love Beryl would have wanted—but did not have—from her father. So the father she remembered from that moment on had a "rough" face; it was the detail that brought him completely alive for me.

It's not really true, of course (though maybe it is), but it does often seem that characters have their own existence beyond you. My first hint of this came when I was a young writer and novelist Fred Chappell said of some dialogue I'd written that I'd "misheard" what the characters were saying.

In the years since I've found that the indication of real life in characters is when they talk on their own. My characters tend to become voluble after I think I've finished writing for the day. I may be in the car doing errands and have to start scribbling down dialogue on my checkbook at a traffic light. A full-blown conversation may take shape when I'm at the Y, swimming laps; I've learned to keep a notebook at the end of the pool.

One time when I mentioned this experience while giving a talk, someone asked me—smiling, but obviously really wondering—what was the difference between me listening to my characters talk and a psychiatric patient who "hears voices."

When personal demons beset a writer the result is usually silence rather than conversation. The infamous writer's block, when there is nothing but the blank page and silence is—for me—caused by harpies I'm not quite hearing. Once when I'd been stuck on a book for a long time, I decided to write what was in my head beyond the apparent blankness. Out poured the carping voices: you call yourself a *writer?* That first book of yours was just a fluke. You can't write this awful stuff down anyway, a nice girl like you. What would your editor say? Your mother? I silenced these demons by making them into characters, giving them names, physical characteristics, clothes, gestures; they'd already provided their own dialogue. I put them into the book and they shut up. Then—sweet revenge—I excised them from the text and they haven't bothered me since.

Another kind of silence occurs when a neglected character, like a spurned lover, gives you the cold shoulder. This often happens to me when I have a particularly busy semester of teaching. I may sit down to write—finally—one Saturday morning and find that the characters have gone vague on me. "They flee from me who some-times did me seek," the first line of a Thomas Wyatt love poem, comes to my mind at such times. They want my attention, it's clear. I vow to get up earlier, spend an hour a day with them, get reac-quainted. Then how eagerly and vividly they will (usually) return.

But sometimes a character goes, or stays, sullenly flat. I have found that in almost all cases this is a matter of not knowing him or her well enough. Just as an unloved child will not thrive, an unknown character will not come to life. It is time, as Melville said, to "mine deeper." At this point, I put the novel aside and begin to write a history of my character's life. Sometimes to get started I use an artificial device, a list of things to consider about a character. From a *Writer's Digest* article that someone gave me years ago I've developed a list that I—and my students—have been using and adding to ever since. The categories include such things as the character's nickname, scars (physical and emotional), hobbies, books read, favorite foods, physical ailments, phobias, contents of dresser drawers, experiences in school, relationships with parents, siblings, cousins, friends. . . . The list could be endless, but by the time I'm well into it I can put it aside because the character has come to life. The most important kind of details are the odd, particular ones that make this person like no other; until I have those, and the heart of the character's problem—what does the character want, what stands in her way—I don't know her well enough to go on. Much of the information I've discovered won't show up on the page but some of it will, often in surprising ways; even more important, my belief in the character, that belief without which writing fiction is impossible, will have firmly taken root.

By the time a character becomes a separate, viable being, I have usually developed a fierce attachment to him or her. I'm bonded, hooked; I'll follow anywhere. One character decided to keep bees. OK, I knew nothing about bees, but I read up on apiculture, virtually every book in the university library and joined the county beekeepers association, where I learned firsthand about hives, queens, drones, bee dances, cures for stings, bee diseases, even bee moods. I discovered unexpected things—that beekeepers (not unlike writers) try to understand the objects of their attention; in the words of one beekeeper (and then my character) they learn to "think like a bee."

Last summer I went to Japan in search of some characters in progress, two of whom lived through the bombing of Hiroshima. With two guides and translators who entered the spirit of my quest I looked at archival pictures and films; talked to a painter who re-creates on canvas scenes of prewar Hiroshima; walked through the streets of Koi, a section of the city where my characters lived, studying the stone walls that were there before the war, and then climbed the steep hill—as some survivors did after the bombing—to Mitaki Temple, a green sanctuary high above the city. I had read accounts of many survivors, but it was only by talking to some of them—including one who told her story for the first time—that I was able to begin to imagine what had seemed unimaginable.

The flowering of characters results in an interesting paradox. It's when a character comes to life in a writer's mind that the character begins to act on his or her own. A completely predictable character is not worth writing about; there is nothing to learn. Such a character probably lacks the kind of complexity that the interesting people in our lives possess. As an exasperated friend of mine once said, after complaining about certain aspects of her husband that continually baffled her, "But what if you knew everything a guy was going to say or do? Wouldn't you just *leave?*"

Some characters, I must admit, I love more than others. Many novelists have had the experience of being so attached to a particular character that they put off writing the scene—for months, even years—in which that character dies or meets with harm. But even the characters I don't love in that way I feel committed to; it's till death, or the completion of the book, do us part. For me perhaps the writing of novels is more like a string of marriages than of love affairs.

Whether the central character in a novel must be lovable or even sympathetic is a question that is often debated. I say no. What a character needs is to be interesting, complex, and to be involved in something important, some issue that matters. I would find it hard to write a novel in which there was no sympathetic central character, yet I can't imagine really getting to know a "villainous" character and not feeling entirely engaged.

In spite of all the terrible things human beings do to each other every day, there are few people who, if really understood, would still seem entirely evil. I have found helpful an exercise that Gail Godwin offered in a workshop: Take a character you hate; write about that person from the outside. Next write about that person from the inside, his point of view. Sometimes I ask my students to do this; they find it the hardest—and often most rewarding—of their assignments. One particularly gifted young writer wrote a brilliant, scathing portrait of a tyrannical professor. She was furious when I asked her to do part two of the exercise, but after fuming a while, she began to develop a rich and fascinating story, the inner life of someone who was not quite the professor she knew, but not entirely unlike him either. The end result was a fine story—and a little more sympathy for the man who inspired it.

If I'm working with a character who is villainous in a flat way I also use Godwin's exercise, trying not only to add my understanding of this person's history but to give him or her something of myself, one of my own less admirable traits, perhaps—the latter a suggestion from novelist Laurel Goldman, who says she puts some part of herself into every character. The result of this work is usually a character who though still thoughtless, cruel, or violent, is more complex, rounder, more believable.

Revenge is a common, and powerful, motive for writing fiction; anger or hurt caused by unhappy childhoods, failed marriages, or love affairs has fueled countless novels. Writing fiction, as Nora Ephron (author of *Heartburn*) has said, is revision—not only writing the scenes over and over until they're fully polished, but a re-vision, a reliving of life, doing it over, coming to terms. The more completely the writer understands the villains of her piece, those characters who have evolved from the enemies in her real life, the stronger the book, and the more she'll learn.

Though characters obviously can't love you back in the same way that a lover or friend in real life can do, I have found that most of my characters whether sympathetic or not often give me something valuable: they teach me what it was I didn't know I knew. Exactly what, I (like my character Sister Agatha, alluding to another subject) do not care to say, but I can say that I emerge from a novel a slightly altered person. Sometimes demons have been exorcised, and along the way I may have learned something about myself that changes the way

I behave in everyday life. And those characters who've helped me toward this have become part of my emotional landscape of friends, relatives, kin.

One of my closest writing friends was a man with whom I shared a love of characters. His name was Lawrence Rudner, author of the novels *The Magic We Do Here* and *Memory's Tailor* and a number of fine short stories. I first met him through Felice, when he reviewed that book and understood my wish to bring to life a world unknown to me except through the imagination. His passion as a novelist was recreating the world of the Polish Jews before they, in his words, "disappeared in a mist." The endings of the novels were by necessity tragic, but the lives of his characters before they were silenced were full of life, humor, and warmth.

Almost every semester Larry read to my fiction writing classes, and sometimes he'd call me into his office to read me a just-completed scene. His physical presence was strong; he had dark eyes, a full beard, large hands and arms—a peasant's body, in the words of another of his friends. Yet it's his voice I remember best, and the delight he took in his characters. Each time he read a scene it was as though for the first time, with the characters surprising him all over again; sometimes he had to wipe away tears of laughter with the heel of his hand. He is gone now, dead from brain cancer at much too young an age, but I can still hear his voice and the voices of Moishe Turkov, his golden-haired, miraculous son Chaim, and Alexandr Davidowich Berman, the tailor who kept memories of forgotten Jews alive. I think Larry would be pleased that I remember him this way, in the company of his characters.

THE CREATIONS OF WATER AND LIGHT

LINDA HOGAN

At night when the ocean is full
of its own created light, the luminescent eel,
the manta ray, the swimming together
minions of the small. At night
when we are carried in the waters of this world
that existed before any of the gods
created earth-light or winged creatures,
I look through the relative darkness
and see the fire of plankton around your body
in the pure grace of shining light.

Fire and water are two elements
unlikely to join. Still, one sometimes comes of the other
as when the body creates its waters
from the fire of sexual yearning
and when the ocean reveals her light-bearing creatures
in the silken water that carries us.

At night when the ocean is teeming with eggs
some creature has entrusted to the sea,

I remember how the body goes into itself,
at that moment between breaths
when it seems the tide of the body might pull away
before it comes back again. In the human body,
it is said, the gods of ocean live below the navel
in the muscles that move like waves of their own accord
and when the bodies are pressed together,
skin against skin,
we can say we remember how ocean was formed,
we can say we knew it at the beginning of time,
the first element when something like gods
or makers fell into each other, cell by cell,
cell to cell,
and became something newly created,
boundless and light.

LEFT-HANDED LOVE

TIM GAUTREAUX

UNCLE RENEE

ACROSS THE ROAD from my uncle's fishing camp I sat out in the open-sided wharf shed, kind of a no-nonsense gazebo under a heavy galvanized roof, lined with benches that were part of the building. It was big enough for six people to get in out of the sun. My uncle was there, the biggest, oldest one, because the women had told him to keep me from falling into the bayou. He leaned back against a wood-clad ice chest and put one foot up on the bench, looking at me as though I was the most worthless object he could think of. I looked back and saw a tall man with a stomach riding over a cracking belt. He wore a khaki baseball cap and his skin was faded like an old magazine left under a car's rear windshield for a year. I guessed he'd had brown hair at one time, though it was gone except for a baby-doll-like fringe near the level of his ears. He spat once over the rail into Bayou LaLoutre and said to me, "Timmy, are you good for anything a-tall?" I was eight years old, dull as a glass of skim milk, and it never occurred to me that there could be anything wrong with what an adult told me. It was 1955 and what men said to me was fact. I didn't answer his question, but held out my hand and felt his rocky thumb press a quarter into my palm. Leaving the protection of the iron roof, I set out across the tar road, picking up my bare feet quickly out of the burning goo and feeling the hair on top of my head fire up like filaments in a light bulb. I walked to Judy's Place, a wood and stucco building at the rear of a toe-torturing clam shell parking lot. Inside, the hot air was ginned up by fans roaring in chrome cages. I put the coin on the counter and Miss Judy pushed open a little brown bag and inserted a frosty can of Falstaff from a cooler.

"Does he have an opener, baby?"

"Yes ma'am. Out on the wharf on a string."

"You go straight back, now."

And I did. My uncle tapped the church key twice on the can and then punched a triangle in the top, letting out a sneeze of beery mist that tickled my nose. He took swallow after swallow with his eyes closed, and I saw how strong and how old he was at the same time. My mother was the baby of eight children, and I was the baby of three, so all my relatives were ancient. Uncle Renee had fought in World War I and told stories like he'd won the whole thing by himself. I believed that he did.

He blinked his eyes and shooed me away. "Go run those crab nets if you want something to eat for supper." I ran out onto the wharf carrying a hamper and raised the lines the way he'd taught me, pulling up two and three devil-angry lake crabs in a net and banging them out of the tangle of string into the hamper. I put out six nets because he generally let me have six salted hard-heads from a foul bucket tied under the wharf. I brought the crabs for him to inspect.

"Nice ones," I told him.

"I seen nicer. Throw a sack over 'em before the sun kills them."

"I'll have enough to feed everybody by sundown," I told him.

He looked across the road toward the rambling brickpaper lodge. I could tell he wanted to be somewhere else. "Why can't you swim?" he asked.

I shrugged. No one had taught me yet. I sat next to him and looked at a watch chain which snaked into a little pocket in his khaki pants. "Can you tell me a story?"

He took a long draw on his can and looked across the bayou. "A little boy didn't learn to swim and fell overboard and drowned. Now go down in that skiff and bail out the rainwater with that coffee can."

A barnacle-studded skiff had been tied next to the wharf for years, a peeling cypress thing with oarlocks. I had never seen anyone in it unless they were bailing it out. I stepped down onto the middle seat with the can and went to work. In a half hour I was scraping the bottom of the hull and the sun was taking up the rest. I yelled to Uncle Renee that I was finished and this woke him up. He looked again at the camp across the road and then pulled his watch. He told me to run the traps. When I'd finished, my forefingers burning from the salt water on the twine, he gave me a quarter for another Falstaff and told me that when I got back I had to finish the boat.

"It's dry," I said.

"Flip open that hatch in the middle and bail that out."

Back from Judy's Tavern, I got down into the slimy bottom and opened a compartment in which there was four inches of water. I bailed it for a few minutes, and it would have taken an idiot not to notice that the water level was not going down. Looking up, I saw Mr. Felix Chambers, a white-haired, bent stump of a man, join my uncle on the wharf bench to help him watch me. I took thirty cans of water out of the compartment and looked up at the men. My head coming up at them must have been some signal, because they both began laughing aloud and pointing at me. "Bail faster, boy, or you'll sink," Mr. Chambers said in his buzzy old voice.

I looked into the water and saw holes in the bottom of the compartment and little currents rising to the surface. "This part of the boat has a leak," I called, and the men laughed harder. I put down the coffee can and smiled back at them because I figured if they were laughing at me, I must deserve it, and it was the right thing to do.

My father loafed across the road and was filled in on the fun. He pushed back his cap, looked in my direction and smiled, but said without laughing, "That's a bait well, boy. You can't bail it out."

I swung the hatch shut and climbed back on the wharf, which was bubbling creosote in the sun. Walking into the group of men I put my hand in my father's baggy triple-stitch jeans to try and find a dime for a soft drink. Mr. Chambers ran his whispery fingers through my hair like he was trying to rub it all off and Uncle Renee swatted my seat once, catching my eye and thumbing a coin at me. I took it and didn't thank him. I remembered they liked to play tricks on each other, and I felt they were letting me join in their hurtful way of playing. I didn't think this, but I looked in their faces and maybe remembered sitting in one of their laps as a five-year-old while they were swilling beer and telling stories, my ear pressed to a chest resonating with a tale, hearing about Mr. Chambers surviving a boiler explosion, my father jumping overboard with a hatchet to chop a towline out of his tugboat's propeller, or Uncle Renee talking about being shot up in the war in France. There was something about hurt that brought people into a group.

MY UNCLE'S CAMP was south of New Orleans on a three-digit highway that dead-ended about a mile past his door, almost in the Gulf. The place was high up on stilts to keep it out of the storm tides and covered in tan brickpaper. Inside was made of painted plywood and planks. A big center room held a potbelly stove and a tall upright piano, painted chairs, a long plain table, and a tarnished brass chandelier above it. On either side of this area were the bedrooms: men, married or single, slept on the left, women on the right. Most things were painted a pale, dusty green. At this time in my life, my parents brought me down there once a month, sometimes more.

The winter of the same year I bailed out the bait well, I was up early, dipping toast in chicory coffee that was half sugar and Pet milk. Uncle Renee came in from the men's side with his browned-out Parker 16-gauge under his arm and a handful of paper shotshells. "Good morning, Mrs. Breaux," he said to my aunt Edna, his wife. Then he looked down at me as though sizing me up yet again. "Go put on your coat, Timmy." When an adult told me to do that, I just did it and then fell in behind whoever gave the order.

We went down the back steps and there he let me drop the shells into the two barrels of the shotgun, a piece engraved on the side plates with scenes of a dog flushing a partridge out of a shock of grass. We walked back to the fence at the edge of the property, and he went through a show of unloading the gun and telling me how to go through five strands of barbed wire and how to help him do the same. Then we were in a noisy, frost-killed cutgrass that ran flat as a lake for many miles. Here and there were ditches which Uncle Renee told me were irrigation lanes left over from when the land grew sugar cane a hundred years before. We walked for a long time, and I could see nothing but his long back because the marsh was taller than I was. The black water that came up in his footprints smelled faintly of rotten eggs. We walked into a ridge of live oaks and out again. Finally, along one of the drainage ditches he stooped and motioned for me to come close. In the depression, fifty feet ahead, a goofy marsh hen picked through the water with her beak. I couldn't believe it when the old man handed over the gun. He positioned the stock against my shoulder, supported the heavy barrel with his left hand, and told me to shoot. Before I cocked one of the fancy hammers, he put a hand on my back and whispered, "Wait just a minute," and he drew from his jacket a salt shaker from the right pocket and a pepper shaker from the left. He took the shotgun and slowly set its butt on the ground, looking me in the eye with great seriousness. "When you're way back in the woods and you have to survive off the game you shoot, always carry salt and pepper on you." I nodded, though I didn't understand. Then he reached up and shook a little salt into the right barrel, followed by a dash of pepper. "This way," he told me, "when you shoot your game, you season it at the same time." I thought my uncle was the cleverest man in the world. A few seconds later I laid low both the marsh hen and myself as the gun knocked me onto my behind.

At the property line fence he showed me how to clean the bird and told me to have Aunt Edna throw it into the stew with the chicken she was cooking for lunch. I plucked the bird and didn't look at my uncle as he told about how he'd shot grouse flying over the trenches in the Argonne forest. Knocked them down with a water-cooled machine gun. In the kitchen I handed my aunt the little carcass and told her, "Don't put no more pepper and salt on this, because it's already seasoned." She gave me a blank stare, then looked out the side window where Uncle Renee was passing below, his Parker broken open over his shoulder. "Honey," she said, "did Uncle put pepper in his gun?" I nodded. "Well, you mustn't ever do that, hear? You'll blow yourself up putting things in a gun barrel."

"But he said . . ."

"He played a joke on you." She dropped the marsh hen into a cast-iron pot holding a raft of chicken parts and pulled off a stove lid, placing the pot onto the open wood flame. "Sometimes the men are mean, baby. I don't understand it."

Just then my father walked through the back door in a wash of cool air, carrying a small boat propeller. I told him about the bird in the pot and he laughed and shook his head, walking on into the big room. From his reaction I guessed everything was all right. I was glad my uncle had spent the whole morning with me. The salt and pepper thing I would tell my friends at school.

MR. LAWRENCE

Every weekend Uncle Renee would invite to his camp a friend from work down at the Illinois Central freight office to come to his camp. Mr. Lawrence was a wrinkled-up rail of a man who'd recently been cured of tuberculosis. He was always lost in whatever clothes he wore, and his eyes were little, as though shrunken by some old and terrible pain. I never saw him do anything unusual other than sit on the floor at night next to the upright piano and keep rhythm with my uncle's playing by dragging an inverted broom handle over the rough floor boards. He was the kind of man who fit his rhythms in with other people's music, the kind who laughed but never caused laughter.

Mr. Lawrence always brought a shiny, skinny-barreled double shotgun with him during the winter, a .410-gauge with elaborately engraved hammers and sidelocks, a Damascus design running down the barrels like interlocking baby curls, and inlays of silver wire on the frame. He saw me admiring it one day and sidled over by the potbelly stove, took it from against the wall and put it in my hands. "Come on," he said. "The back yard's full of robins."

"Can you eat robins?" I asked.

"Nothing better if you wrap 'em in bacon and simmer that in a covered skillet." He wore two old brown jackets, though I don't remember the day being especially cold. We walked under the camp to sneak up on the birds, and by the back steps near the dripping cistern he handed me two green shells made of fluted cardboard. I could hold the little gun up by myself and aim it. He put his wobbly little head next to mine. "You're just a boy, so you can nail those birds on the ground. But when you grow up, you should step out and let them fly. It's more sporting when they have a chance. Then you'll shoot the ones going up and away so the pellets can get under their feathers. You don't want to make any cripples if you can help it." I let fly with one barrel and then the other, bowling over two birds. After I picked those up, more robins flew in, and I missed those. We sat in the shadow on two rusty Jerry cans, saying nothing, watching robins drift in by twos. The dark solid artwork sat in my lap like an iron jewel. When he'd point, I'd draw back the two hammers and shoot. Soon we had enough to fill a pot, and when he put out his skeletal hand, I placed the narrow gun into it and turned to deal with the birds. He struggled up the steps and that was the last time I ever saw him.

MR. BABIN

At the end of the highway was Mr. Babin's tavern, a little stucco dance hall on the edge of the marsh. The owner was a dark, thick man who liked children. His bad luck was that children were afraid of him. Mr. Babin had no arms. They'd been burned off when he'd come in contact with live wires during his job as an electrician, and on his stumps were crab-like chrome-plated pincers. When I was drinking a Grapette or a Nesbit at the bar (country taverns admitted children in those days) he would come up behind me and take the whole top of my ear in his mouth and bite it. I'd jump down and run off a few feet, and everyone at the bar would laugh. I'd wipe my ear dry and Mr. Babin would reach out with his left prosthesis, his stronger one, a quarter pinched in the chrome vise. "Hey, play us some music," he'd say, and then watch me try to jerk the quarter free as he clamped down. I'd always go after the coin because the jukebox gave six plays for a quarter and I could spend a half hour making selections, one of which would always be "The Legend of Davy Crockett." When the coin scraped free, he'd pretend to bite me again and I'd run off. Sometimes he'd come up to my father and me and put a plastic arm on my shoulder in a way that made me think that when he was a young man, he'd had a kid or two himself. I didn't like Mr. Babin, but I remember a night at the camp when one of my arms fell asleep under me in bed, and the lack of feeling woke me up. I reached over with my wooden arm and put it on my snoring father to see what it was like not to feel people.

MR. SKEETS

His real name was Elmo Keenan and he was sixty-nine years old, never without shined brown-leather lace-ups, ironed gray slacks, and a clean, starched shirt. His face was lean and unlined, his iron-colored hair he kept slicked back to his skull, and even to an eight-year-old he seemed young. He laughed at everything, a kind of staccato bray given through his arched nose, and the more Prager beer he drank on a hot day, the more he laughed. He drove a gray 1939 Plymouth that in 1955 was showroom-new. Mr. Skeets must have been born smiling, and I remember that at night, when he and everyone else went down to Babin's, the ladies he danced with smiled, too, and his leather shoes slid like they were gliding on butter as he fox-trotted in the glow of a Wurlitzer jukebox, heels never touching the floor. I didn't know feet could do that.

For firewood, Uncle Renee brought used lumber and pallets from the city's railroad yards, which had to be cut to short lengths in afternoon sawing-and-beer-drinking sessions. It was always my job to cut kindling for the camp's stoves, and I made enough racket to wake everybody up bamming the little planks with a hatchet as they lay flat on the floor. Mr. Skeets rose early one morning and came near the stove, putting a hand on my arm.

"Timmy," he said through his nose. "You know what grain is in wood?" I didn't know the word. "See these lines?" he ran a crooked ivory-colored finger over a short length of cypress one-by-six. "That's grain." He took the hatchet from me, stood the board on the floor and tapped it with the blade. A strip of kindling plinked against the wall. I was amazed. "Never cut against the grain, cut with it," he told me, sending another half-inch-wide stick spinning away. He took my Band-Aid-covered left hand and placed it in the middle of the left side of the board and gave me the hatchet. "Put your hand down here and you won't nick it anymore." After a few tries I got the hang of it, and in ten minutes had made enough kindling for two days' fires. My aunt Edna brought him a cup of coffee and he sat there watching me. "There, you learnt yourself a trade," he said and laughed like a mule.

It might have been that same weekend that I'd brought in my Red Ryder BB gun and left it on the big table under the dusty chandelier, cocked. Later in the day Mr. Skeets came up, when I walked in from the yard, and asked me if I had left my gun cocked. He wasn't smiling. I lied and said no. He began to give me a little kindly lecture about not leaving loaded or cocked guns around, and I started to move off toward the kitchen, not paying attention, but he took his hand from behind his back and held out to me a thumb with a red ditch the width of a BB cut deep across the back of it. "I picked up that gun to move it." I turned away from what I had caused and didn't say a thing to him, not even later when I found him in the workshop pouring turpentine on the wound and wiping it clean with his white linen handkerchief.

MR. ALMEDA

Sometimes the men would gather after lunch in Judy's Place, a bar/cafe three camps down from my uncle's. Judy's husband, Felix, was a retired steam tug pilot and he and my father, Minos, who in those days was an active river captain, would swap stories and argue. One afternoon Mr. Felix began telling in his sandpapery voice how, before short-wave radios were invented, he could make his steam whistle talk a language to other tug pilots. Daddy countered with the time he'd put his hand in the crankcase of a tugboat engine to feel for a hot journal and the wheelman hit the air starter, causing a rod-cap nut to pull his wedding ring into the shape of a teardrop. Then Mr. Felix took his cap off his frosty hair, threw it on the table, and told how he was in the wheelhouse of the old catamaran ferry at Esplanade Avenue when the Bisso tug *Sipsey* came out of a fog bank and went between the hulls, cutting the vessel in half. Daddy reminded him that Bisso didn't own the *Sipsey*, Coyle Lines did, and Uncle Renee yelled from the bar that the *Sipsey* was renamed the *Barranca* before she hit the ferry, and Mr. Felix cursed them both and yelled that he was in the wheelhouse, not them, when the tug's smokestack crashed through the front windows and it was a red stack with a yellow band painted on it, not a white stack like a Coyle Line boat, and then Daddy hollered that Whiteman Towing Company had the white stacks, and things went downhill from there. It was like that just about every time they told stories.

Mr. Almeda was famous for not saying anything during these matches. He was a husky medium-brown Spaniard with a whispery Latin voice, a man never loud, never angry or disdainful. Even Mrs. Judy would get into the discussions with the men, if only to to quiet them down, but Mr. Almeda would resettle his cap on his wavy white hair which was patterned like the border frosting on a birthday cake, and smile his separateness.

His little wharf was close to my uncle's, and sometimes, when I was playing by the bayou bank, one of the women would call over to him to keep an eye on me. I watched him unload his catch of crabs one afternoon, late, as he counted them into wooden hampers for the buyer who came by around sundown. His favorite joke was to reach out with the wooden crab-grabber and seize my ankle with it. "I'm gonna put you in the box and ship you to New Orleans with the boy crabs," he said. I asked him if there were boy crabs and girl crabs. He said, "What you talkin', Timmy. You don't know the difference?" Mr. Almeda was amazed anybody couldn't tell one from the other, so he sat Indian-style on the wharf planks, showing the horny bottoms of his bare feet. "Look at that." He showed the difference between males and females on the outside, showed me a female bursting with millions of eggs and told me what she did with them. He found two dead crabs in his catch and pulled off their shells, showing me the differences inside the two sexes, which was big news to me, and made me wonder about the ample insides of my aunts. Then one by one, he took crabs from his catch box and let me see the differences, how one was fat, one nearly empty, one ready to become a soft-shell—busters, he named them. There was a one-season crab, a two-season crab, a lake crab, a deep-water crab which had a clean shell, a crab which was rusty-colored from living in a certain lagoon, a crab from southern Lake Borgne which was stained with crude oil, and so on, telling me, within a mile, where each spent its life, and how much it had fought. "Somebody can look at a hamper of crabs and say they all look the same, but they just like people. All you got to do is look good." He pulled out a big fellow, which must have been fourteen inches claw to claw, and showed me how to put him to sleep by rubbing his belly. "This crab, he's like your Uncle Renee. He thinks he's a big shot." Mr. Almeda laughed a whispery laugh.

"He killed the Germans in France," I said.

The old man smiled and threw the crab into his personal hamper to boil for supper. "Your Uncle got to Paris the day the peace treaty was signed. Boy, you got to watch people so you can tell when they saying the truth. In the eye, that's where you got to look 'em."

I didn't like what he was telling me, so I walked across the hot road to the camp and went inside. Uncle Renee and Mr. Chambers were nailing an animal hide to the women's bathroom door. I put out my hand and felt the short fur.

"That's a bear hide," my uncle said. "I was in the back yard taking out the trash when he attacked me from behind." I looked carefully at the hide, which was the color of a light brown cow. "What happened?"

"Well, Mr. Skeets came up with that bayonet I keep in the kitchen drawer, and he jumped on the bear's back. Killed him with one stab right to the heart." He brought a fist down into his palm, and I glanced at his eyes, then looked back at the door a long time. I think he thought I was bored, trapped out in the woods with old people, nobody my age to play with. He was trying to make his camp exciting for me, for he and all the men and women loved the place like a priest loves Rome.

Late that night when I was in bed, it was too hot to sleep, and through the salt-dripping screen I heard Mr. Almeda walking in the road, coming from Judy's, and he was singing something in Spanish, his voice soft as cotton in the damp night, and I thought of the short-haired bears waiting for him in the roadside brush.

UNCLE NOLAN

My mother's brother left Louisiana during World War I to find work and wound up in the Merchant Marine. He was always in China, gone for months and years at a time, so the family got used to not seeing him. One time he was in San Francisco, fresh off a long voyage, a big payoff in his pocket, when he was hit on the head, robbed, and left in the street. For a long time, years, I understood, he didn't know who he was. Finally, a former shipmate noticed him in a soup kitchen, staring at an empty plate as though the greatest mystery in the world was in his reflection in the glazing. His friend walked over and put a hand on him and said, "Nolan." Uncle Nolan said, "Who?"

Eventually, the family got him back to New Orleans and he lived with Uncle Renee and Aunt Edna in their big house on South Pierce Street. I'm not sure he ever remembered who he was, but the family told him enough for him to think of himself as this person, Nolan Adoue, and that's how he lived. He was short and thin, liked to do chores, I guess because he was trained to keep busy on ships. When he came to the camp, he didn't drink and make noise like the other men. I remember him always in the background, soft-spoken and helpful, no wry smiles at the foolishness around him, always working carefully at something. One night when I didn't feel like going out in the cold to watch the adults dance and talk, I was left at the camp alone with him. He cleaned up the kitchen and then sat at the table and talked with me as if I were an adult. I showed him a corroded old V-nickel I'd gotten from my Aunt Vivian, and he took me to the sink and showed me how to remove the reddish discoloration. He scrubbed the nickel with cream of tartar and vinegar for a long time, until the metal was bright and I could read the date, 1889. I put the coin in my pocket and went to bed, leaving him to wait up for the adults, so he could clean up after them. That was the last I remember of him. Later that winter he was sawing up stove wood in the side yard and Aunt Edna opened the window in the room behind the kitchen and asked him, "Nolan, do you want some fresh coffee?" He looked up and told her, "Yes, that would be fine." She walked into the kitchen, poured him a cup, added cream and sugar, and walked back to the open window to see her brother lying on the ground, dead of a stroke. I was in the front yard when it happened and didn't learn or feel a thing. All I knew is that we had to leave the camp early, go into town, and prepare for a funeral, and I was angry at this trouble. I didn't understand the women's tears. As far as I knew, Uncle Nolan hadn't been much of a presence in anyone's life, and though he knew my name, he didn't even know who he was.

CHILDHOOD IS A time when "thank you" is an unknown phrase, or if used at all, is as meaningless as a doorbell rung by a prankster. Old people know that children are incapable of love, that love is a learned thing. They know it takes people their whole lives to find out that love is doing something for folks who might never do anything for you. When people get old and ramble in the big lagoon of time after their own children have left and their work life is coming to an end, they have as many hours to waste as children do, and days to begin learning again, and teaching as well. Shortly after my parents stopped going to that marshlands camp, around the time I was fourteen, Mr. Lawrence died, then Mr. Babin, followed by Mr. Almeda. Uncle Renee died in the Illinois Central Hospital, a rundown nightmare of a place, and though I was driving past there one day on the expressway and could see the ancient brick facade, I decided I didn't want to waste my time to go and see him. Old as he was when I knew him, I think Mr. Skeets outlived everybody, laughing through his nose in his little wooden house off St. Claude Avenue.

Not one of them got a thanks from me, though I learned from them how to tell a story, how to dance smooth and shoot fair, how to laugh and enjoy children, how to look closely at everything and everybody, how never to go against the grain of wood or anything else, and finally, when I remember Uncle Nolan lying in the yard, the thought of a sweet cup of dark roast coffee fading like a spark in his brain, how to understand what being alive means. I wonder if the old folks realized, before they gave it, that I wouldn't appreciate their time and attention, or if they had lived so long that they understood they were planting seeds for a garden they would never enjoy.

WHISPERS

MYRA GOLDBERG

WEDDINGS

THERE WAS WILDNESS at those weddings. Dancing Chassidim carried the bride and groom, like gymnasts, on their shoulders, and the newlyweds met in air while a band played strange and familiar music. The wedding guests were strange and familiar, too. They had the Goldberg nose and my father's Polish-German accent, but were thicker in the waist than we were, wearing cocktail dresses or black Chassidic garb instead of shirtwaists and blue suits. What was strange and grew familiar, wedding after wedding, were the grown-ups, standing by the silver lions spewing punch, whispering "... numbers on his arms, ... hidden in a cave ... the Poles ... in the attic ... dead ... alive."

Those weddings came home to Westchester with me, filled with music and life, shadowed by death and savagery. There, riding my bike or playing Hide and Go Seek in the suburban twilight, imaginary Germans chased me, as they'd chased my relatives in Poland. If I'd hated those weddings or been cool towards my family instead of loving them, I don't think those whispers would have shaped my life and its choices in the same way. For it is love that makes room inside us for the details to enter and what we love enters as details: silver lion fountains, and passionate wailing music, and whispers of something too serious to name. "We think in generalities, but we live in specifics," my father, whose home town was five miles from Auschwitz, told us.

BROWN VERSUS THE BOARD OF EDUCATION

Each April lilacs bloomed in my aunt's backyard in time for my grown cousin's birthday party. Then in 1954, the Supreme Court outlawed segregation in the nation's schools and the party became a celebration for both the birth and the decision.

My uncle, a Communist, managed a Harlem liquor store, and his salesmen, tall brown men in immaculate suits with blazing white shirts and gold cufflinks, appeared in the garden among the lilacs. The men laughed a lot and kidded me, a little girl, and carried opalescent glasses full of gin and tonic around as Billie Holiday sang "Hush now, don't explain." My brothers and I wandered in and out of the house, playing Haitian drums in a dazzling white room that my aunt, a painter, had made into a gallery, thirty years before Soho. Here, as in Brooklyn, I fell in love with something whole, whose details were erotic, smelling like lilacs and gin and beautiful brown men and art and bohemianism. All of which, I felt vaguely, had something to do with *Brown versus*, as if the presence of those men and that music in my uncle's backyard had both caused the justice's decision and arisen from it.

OUR BABIES COME IN SEVERAL COLORS

Thirty years later, I sat in a lawyer's office answering questions. I'd spent my youth protesting the Vietnam war, writing, marrying, un-marrying, and now, after years of yearning for a child and trying to conceive, I was ready to adopt. The lawyer's office was professional, neither wild, erotic, nor aesthetic, with ugly anonymous paintings on white walls.

"What kind of child do you want?" the lawyer held up his pen expectantly.

An odd question asked by a bland stranger in an ugly room, but I'd already considered the answer, I thought. Older children came with problems I found daunting. A child from India or Brazil in-volved acres of red tape.

"A baby," I said. "From this country if possible."

The lawyer, ever accommodating, wrote *infant*. "Health?"

"Healthy, sure, why not. Do I get the choice?"

"You want white? Jewish?" For this he put his pen down.

"A baby," I said, certain and slightly confused, as he explained that white babies were more expensive and harder to get than non-white. As I listened, I saw that I'd barely thought about the question. I'd probably assumed white, but Jewish felt like a cultural rather than biological category, and I'd given up the idea of a child that looked like me. Finding a non-white baby, then, would be easier than finding a white baby, and giving a home to a baby who really needed one would be more gratifying than competing for one, but beyond these factors, I thought, babies are babies, and only Nazis think they are anything else. (Earlier on, doing artificial insemination, when the lab matched me with a Russian, Jewish, flute-playing donor, I felt pleased, as if I were marrying the man, instead of borrowing his sperm. But adoption was about babies who already existed or almost existed.)

The lawyer made a note on the file, which he shoved to one

side. "We won't have to advertise. If you're willing to take a baby that's African American and something else, there's an agency in Texas I can call. I'll get back to you tomorrow."

Later, standing in a coffee bar, stirring foaming cappucino, I felt exhausted, as if I'd done something momentous, without being clear about exactly what it was. I kept returning to my inability to specify ethnicity or race. It was no mystery. Those weddings. Those relatives. People dividing babies into those that lived and those that got gassed because they were Jewish.

Walking home, I peeked in baby carriages. Sure enough, babies came in all colors. Although on this block, the mothers seemed to match. Relief pervaded my walk home, and excitement. I'd been spared the need to advertise my yearnings to strangers, and this baby would need my home. "You're aware that this child might not be Charles Darwin," said the nice liberal therapist I'd been seeing about this decision. "He may not even be college material." Startled, I said, "But maybe he'll be Charlie Mingus or Charlie Parker," feeling startled and silly.

The lawyer called back. "The birth mother is Pentacostal. A white girl. Eighteen, nineteen years old. The birth dad's in the Air Force, African American, married with kids. Everyone seems healthy. He repairs airplanes. Call her. See what you think."

The papers held a picture of a pretty girl with big hair and lots of mascara with a family history of the ordinary: an occasional heart attack, overweight, downward mobility. Her great-grandfather had been the mayor of a tiny midwestern town. Her mother was a housekeeper in a motel. The girl had a ninth-grade education and answered the phone at Jack in the Box. There was no information about the father's family. I looked at the phone number, dizzy with anticipation. Then I paid the Gods with worry: was this irresponsible? Racism was real, if race as a category was not. How would my child be prepared for this world, if I could only mutter about Parker and Mingus?

What about her identity? Still, a real woman was awaiting my call, with a real baby coming soon who needed a family.

"I'm white, her dad is black," said the young woman on the phone from Texas. "I was in school in Kentucky with lots of black kids. I figure they're just like us, only darker. Met her dad at a dance, he was married, only I didn't know it, he took me to visit his grand-mother without telling me about the wife or kids. But when I said I was pregnant, he said, 'I'll believe it when there's proof,' can you beat that? He got shipped out to Panama afterwards. It broke my heart. I didn't have a father myself. I've torn up all his pictures. A big man. Very dark. Has six brothers, all preachers, a nice man, funny, with a good heart. How could he do this to me and the baby?

"We're Pentacostal, we don't believe in abortion, my family, tell the truth, it's been in my mind to tell you this, they want me to do this, but I prayed and prayed to make sure this was right for the baby and not just for me. Then I talked to the counselor the agency sent. I want to give this baby a better life than I can manage. But it's been hard finding anyone, and the time is getting closer, so I was glad when they told me about you.

"I want her to know that I loved her, that I did this for love. Will you tell her that?"

I talked to her again. She was straightforward, emotional, direct. We talked about my neighborhood, job, plans for the baby's care and her romance, disappointment, future. She sounded like one of my college students, minus the middle-class diction, and the sense of entitlement. I fantasized about her getting a scholarship at the college where I taught. She mentioned that she'd love to see New York.

Then we both jumped back into our roles, the professor in her forties, who didn't know if this girl would change her mind about the baby, and a girl waiting to deliver a baby to a stranger.

I prepared for a baby with a passed-down crib, tiny sheets, and Penelope Leach. Then I talked to a black friend, Willie, who said,

"Listen, if she's light-skinned, your kid's life won't be too different from if she were a little exotic, say Jewish, but if she's dark . . . well, never mind, she probably won't be."

GETTING ANNA

The chapel in Austin was dim, but I could make out a weeping child holding a baby in her arms. It was the birth mother, looking like an Appalachian Virgin Mary, with the baby, looking like a large pink and white doll with black hair.

"I wanted to hand her to you, Myra," said the tearful child, flanked by her neat, smiling sister and a neutral-looking social worker.

I have two pictures of that moment. A tearful, plump American child stands beside a sympathetically sad older woman with a Semitic face. First one holds the baby, then the other. The baby is crying, as the sister announces that she weighs ten pounds. Then I'm feeding her, awkwardly. "They'll take her back if I don't seem more competent," I think.

"I've told Anna the story," said the birth mother gravely. "I know she heard me."

She wept some more. Tears came to my eyes. The baby went on crying. Everyone else smiled and shuffled their feet. Later, I took Anna to the ladies' room so the birth mother could leave the hospital without seeing us and feeling worse. "Oh, the ten-pound one is yours," said a woman at the sink. I left the bathroom feeling I'd stolen this baby instead of adopting her. I deposited her in a car seat for the trip to the motel: this small stranger, whom I'd invited into my life for the rest of her life and mine, sat, strapped in beside me. "This is too bizarre," I thought, lifting her out and carrying her into the motel, feeling shell-shocked.

I have been told by mothers of first children that this shell-shocked state is common. That the sudden appearance of a real child in the world, after nine months of pregnancy, strikes one as strange. Certainly a real baby after acres of paperwork, months of visits from a social worker, and trips to a lawyer's office, feels at least as strange. And love, under the circumstances, was the last thing I felt.

In my stupified state, I put the baby, sitting in her car seat, on the rug across the motel room, while I sat on the bed and picked up Ursula Le Guin in paperback. I read a few sentences, as if to reassure myself that I was still me, reader and writer. Then I looked over at her. Babies, especially newborns, often look grave, as if they've come with news from the other side, where the dead and the not-yet-alive reside. This baby was long, sturdy, with a black fringe of hair and a calm, peaceful face. She sat, like some primitive painting, awaiting me. There was a welling up inside, then a thought first detached, then indelible: I could love her. I crossed the room to get her, feeling as if the possibility was a reality now. Love, in this case, felt both involuntary, a kind of tropism, and chosen, as that decision in the lawyer's office had been involuntary and chosen. Then the feeling became part of a practice, a discipline in a difficult world, not love, but loving.

All babies, of course, are strangers, and loving a baby you fall in love with what you glimpse as the sun lights up the face in the cradle and they reach out and smile. Then babies become themselves as you love them. A serious nose appears, then a body style. You smell her, bathe her, comb her hair. She flips off the bed, crawls, talks, walks, talks back to you. A kind of texture or temperament is discernible. This one was both energetic and calm, merry and passionate. No, no, no, she says, at sixteen months, no longer an angel, but a human child. And love, of course, is in the dailiness, the details, the giggling from the high chair, the plump feet, the ecstasy in the swing. While the practice of love is in the learning to mother, the long nights, the ear infections, how to stretch patience, see things through a child's eyes, throw out expectations. Laugh, be firm, be flexible. Buy sugar cereal. Insist on manners and baths. What was special about our situation came from outside us.

First, before I left Texas, the agency called me back. "Down here, we don't take in each other's children," said the social worker obliquely. Then she asked a lot of questions about how discipline was handled in my family. Thinking, apparently, that I might have adopted a biracial child in order to beat her.

"This child isn't biracial," said the pediatrician in New York. "She's got no Mongolian spot. Maybe the birth mother lied to you."

"We get darker as we get older," my black neighbor said, adding to the confusion which is the beginning of knowledge.

Then women, like witches, appeared around the carriage.

"That baby is too cold."

"That baby is too hot."

"Enjoy yourself. It goes like lightning."

"Her father? Is he very . . . tall?"

And as Anna's hair grew curlier and her skin became coffee and cream, children asked: "Are you her real mother?"

Some days I knew I was and some days I wondered.

One day, when she was four, I heard a child from Anna's daycare center, taking a survey: "Were you born or were you adopted?" "Am I a doctor?" responded another four-year-old. Shortly after, some child stated, "You're not Anna's real mother, you don't look anything like her." In a voice that held conviction, I answered, "You're right. We don't look anything like each other, but we are alike inside, because she is my daughter."

Of course, we were and we weren't alike, like everybody else and her daughter.

WHO ARE THE STRANGERS?

Along with a passion for this child and my gratitude for this miraculous gift came a change in how I looked at people. First, I nodded at strollers, their occupants and the people who pushed them. Then, I gazed at black or Hispanic-looking teenagers trying to see how Anna would look later on. Tall with a great pouf of hair on top. The girl in overalls and a backpack. Then I found myself huddling with black mothers at school events, or writing impassioned letters for tenure on behalf of black candidates at school. Black students started choosing my classes, although I had no idea why exactly. I also began looking differently at children Anna's age. Our kids, I thought, exchanging glances with the mothers of color. Then mothers of any kind. For when you adopt outside of the boundaries of biology, you begin to think of yourself as anybody's mother, potentially.

"I AM ASSUMING," I told my neighbor when Anna was five, "this will never happen again."

"Well," he huffed, "if you'd introduced your babysitter to me, I'd have opened the door."

"We've had the same babysitter for years," I said.

The babysitter, a tan Hispanic girl, with gold hoop earrings and tight jeans, was bringing Anna, now Hispanic-looking, home. The neighbor refused to open the front door to them. "Mama, he told his child not to open the door either," said Anna.

So, I saw, my child, when I was along, was one thing, and my child alone or with another person of color was another.

The world kept talking to us. A job appeared in St. Louis, but the town was segregated, I was told. We left a McDonald's because a white man stared so angrily I thought he might take out a gun. My friendly, intelligent child was accepted to a private school and a woman whose child was rejected said, "Well, of course, they must have wanted a black."

"Are African Americans stupid?" Anna called from the living room one evening.

"Where did you get that idea?"

"The radio."

National Public Radio was having a panel discussion on *The Bell Curve.*

"People have a lot of stupid ideas," I said.

But we stayed in my integrated neighborhood and chose a school with lots of middle-class black kids.

"Can't we go live in a big house with a yard like my cousins?" Anna asked one morning.

I pictured us in the suburbs, a gray-haired single mother, with no appliances and three computers, and a lively, African American girl with a head full of blue and white beads.

"I bet we'll live here forever," Anna guessed. "Unless you find something really cheap. And if I can't have a house or a brother or sister, can I have a dog? Please, please, I beg of you, Mama."

We took in a stray black-and-white kitten, lots of goldfish, and an African frog. Anna hung out the window looking for the mother of the stray, whom she called the birth cat.

WHO ARE THE STRANGERS?

"You can't tell me," said a friend, "that when you see a bunch of black boys walking towards you, with those baggy pants and sneakers on, you don't feel scared."

By now a crowd of black babysitters, older brothers, students, and friends had appeared in our lives, some in baggy pants and sneakers. "Try looking at their faces," I finally said. "They all wear the same clothes. But they don't all look or act alike."

"That's all very well," he said. "But I was mugged."

I thought about the people who'd harmed me as this man had been harmed. The abuser in the movie theater, a date rapist, a man climbing through my window. All white. All men. The numbers on my relatives' arms came from Christians. Still, I wasn't scared of men, whites, Christians. True, some of the whispers at those weddings were about good Poles who'd hidden relatives, as that lilac-filled party had been about a good decision, not a bad one. Then I remembered Anna's birth mother, explaining how she got involved with the birth dad by saying, "I went to school with a lot of black kids in Kentucky." Maybe you had to get close enough to people to know the good from the bad ones. This child came to me courtesy of Brown Versus the Board of Education, I thought, smiling as my friend waited for an answer. "You look at their faces instead of their clothes," I said again.

Love for a child, of course, requires endless revisions that are about you and your child and not color or neighbors or court decisions. Despite her pleas, Anna and I live alone with our pets. We are roommates and playmates, as well as family. Sometimes we make deals. She gets *Snow White* from the video store, I get *Modern Times*. Other times, about bedtime, I rule. About sleepovers on weekends, she prevails. This child, like other members of my family, is verbal, energetic, passionate, musical, melodramatic, stubborn. I discover that when I'm tired, the humor and detachment I've learned as a grown-up disappear. I'm up for tenure. A book comes out. She dawdles on the way to school; I drag her by the hand. She interrupts me on the phone when the dean calls; I shove her. She cries, "I hate you, Mom." I hate who I've become. I read books and try patience, walking away. She grows into negotiation. I learn to say no without yelling. Other mothers help. So do other children.

We collect family stories: the time Anna's friend cut Anna's braids off. The time, at three and a half, she was so mad at me that she stuck my favorite hair ornament in her tushy, drew it out, and said, "See what I've done to your favorite thing." Then she is in kindergarten. There is a head lice crisis just as a friend and colleague dies and I'm appointed chair of my department. Out of ignorance and distraction, I send my scratching child to school. The crisis is our fault, say two white parents. One mother goes to the principal. Anna, whose favorite pants have holes in the knees, is a neglected child, she says. The other parent knocks Anna with her elbow as she comes into class, and whispers to the white girls' moms that Anna shouldn't be asked to other children's houses. A black woman calls to recommend hair oils. "We don't get head lice. The lice don't like the smell of the oils. But you really must do something about that hair."

Until then, when Anna yelled that the comb hurt, I backed off. After that, she goes to a hair braider, or the Dominican hairdresser, and I say, "No you can't go to school in your old pants without your hair combed," insisting on things I don't care about for the sake of this child I love. By the end of the year, I resign the chairmanship although I like the power and the chance to change things, because if love is not theoretical, it takes time.

ELIJAH IN A NEW SUIT

There are fewer weddings in our family now, but there are Passovers. The guests tonight are my mother, Anna, her cousins, me, two members of a string quartet, my cousin, who holds us all together, her son, a Jewish rock musician, and his wife, a member of the royal family of Bhutan. We all listen as Pharoah's army gets drowned in the Red Sea, but the real miracle at the table is that my cousin has just returned from the hospital where he has given his kidney to his wife. He is gentle and loving towards her, and I'm struck by how sacrifice can lead to love as well as stem from it, as the little girls run in and out, grabbing macaroons.

"I know you drank Elijah's wine," says Anna, leaning over my shoulder.

I'm disappointed. I was thrilled as a child to feel the prophet Elijah's invisible wings brush by as we stood by the door. In the taxi going home, Anna says that we're allowed to eat with our hands, because her Bhutanese cousins do when they are eating Bhutanese food. "Rice, Ma. They eat rice with their fingers." Then, "Tell me about the ... operation Ma. How do you give someone a kidney? Is it scary? Did it hurt?"

I tell her how D'chen's relative changed her mind about giving her a kidney, how Danny decided to donate his, how they were put to sleep so it didn't hurt. The story sounds like a fairy tale. The deep sleep, the gift of something essential to life. Perhaps Anna is musing on Sleeping Beauty. Or connecting this dreamy story with her birth mother or the smells of lilac on the Passover table, or love, or conviction.

"So," Anna says, leaning against me, "she adopted his kidney. Is that what you call it?"

WHISPERS, AGAIN

At bedtime, Anna likes me to read to her from the book I'm reading. On that Passover Eve: Isaac Babel's journal. It's bloodier than I'm prepared for, filled with Polish pogroms. I close the book. "My father came from that place." Anna knows the story. My father left Poland with his two younger brothers at fifteen to search for his father in America. He was a little like her, I say, Big and smiling and thoughtful. When his brothers got head lice, he shaved their heads and put caps on them, to hide the infection. They found their father on the Lower East Side, I add.

Anna giggles about the lice. Other kids have lice this year, but not her.

I pounce on a lesson: "You know how when you're grumpy, you blame me for everything? Well, in Europe, they said everything was the Jews' fault. Here, sometimes, things are blamed on African Americans."

"Like us," she said, meaning, I guess, that we are African American and Jewish.

"Yes," I said. But the whole business is confusing. She can be Jewish, but I can't be African American, although when someone made a racist remark the other day, I thought, *they think I'm a white person,* as if I might not be. Then I realize I'm a person with African American relatives. As I'd been one with Jewish relatives. People I love.

"You love quiet time," she said. "Cozying up."

I exchanged Babel for *Angelina Ballerina.* It's about a mouse who is really a ballerina.

"You were showing off, today, in the park," she said. "Acting strict in front of those parents."

She's right. I hate other mothers to see me as wishy-washy. But I love the idea that my daughter is wise to me. Love, I've decided, has a lot to do with getting close enough to know someone.

"Zani said you're my stranger mother." She goes on. "Is that true?"

"I'm not your birth mother," I say, "But I am your real mother. Or why would I make you go to bed right this minute." The light goes off, Billie Holiday goes on, and we lie in the dark, cavelike room together, whispering.

''I MISS THE PERSON I LOVE EVERY DAY''

SHAWN WONG

OUR NEW FRIENDS in Rome, Franco and Scilla, are telling my wife Vicki and me that when we finish visiting the main attractions of Rome, we must visit a little thirteenth-century convent and church named Santi Quattro Coronati in the Laterano district of Rome. Its beauty is in its simplicity and its surprises. It is the opposite of the more famous and lavish churches and basilicas of Rome, with their grand facades, stunning marble interiors, Bernini statues, Caravaggio paintings, and Michelangelo ceilings. Franco tells us that the tiny chapels of St. Sylvester and Santa Barbara, on the sides of the main church, will be a complete surprise. But Vicki won't be able to see Santi Quattro Coronati, because she'll be leaving in a few days to return home to Seattle to work, leaving me in Rome for a month with fourteen of my students from the University of Washington.

This marks the second time Vicki and I have been apart for an extended period in the ten years we've been married; the first time, three years ago, I was also in Italy for a month when I was awarded a residency at the Rockefeller Foundation center in Bellagio. Neither one of us takes separation well. We maintained contact then and now by speaking on the phone every day. The technological difference between my two sojourns in Europe is the conquest of Europe by the Internet and the cellular phone. Just prior to coming to Italy, Vicki and I spent a week in Ireland, where one day on the Dingle Peninsula, far in the southwest corner of Ireland, we were stopped on a one-lane road waiting for the sheep to clear the road in front of our car in that classic and stereotypical postcard-pastoral landscape. After a while the sheepherder appeared around the bend speaking on a cellular phone, the dog at his side peering up at him as if waiting to hear what the conversation was about.

At the opposite end of the spectrum, we visited the ancient 5,000-year-old tombs north of Dublin in Knowth and Newgrange in the Boyne Valley and places which bear names like the Mound of Hostages. There is evidence in the stones of a civilization that communicated in symbols. No one is really sure what the symbols mean, but viewing the symbols in relation to the landscape in which they were placed adds meaning, even understanding, without knowledge. The permanence of the tombs and the carvings in stone were obviously meant to communicate something to a civilization long after theirs had passed. I am told the wheel hadn't been invented when these magnificent tombs were built.

After Vicki leaves Rome, I am given an array of communication choices. I have, of course, a telephone in my apartment and I'm told not to dial direct, using the expensive monopoly-driven Italian phone company, but to access a toll-free number and use my telephone credit card. I will be connected instantly with the comforting *bong* of AT&T. The University of Washington staff tells me that I can connect with my university e-mail. I decline. There is express mail, a fax machine, and slower, but reliable, Vatican mail that will get a letter to Seattle in five days. We have e-mail, a fax machine, and two telephone lines at home, a cellular phone in the car; and UPS, FedEx,

Airborne, and DHL drop off mail and packages regularly. All of that is duplicated on a bigger scale at my university office.

By the end of my first week, my plan to simplify my ties to communication technology fails when I call Vicki three times in one day and ask her to fax something. Then I ask someone else to send an e-mail message for me, and finally, I send something by express mail. My only victory is in not actually sending the e-mail myself.

When I write letters these days, it's to convey an idea, to express my thanks, my appreciation, my sympathy, or my congratulations— to construct a piece of writing almost as if the letter were a polished piece of creative writing. I very rarely ask questions in letters these days. Questions are conveyed by e-mail and telephone. "Can you meet for lunch?" "When is the meeting?" "Did you pay my Visa bill?" "What's the weather like there?" "What should I pick up on the way home?" "When will you be home?" "What are you wearing to dinner?" "How was your day?"

I want Vicki to know the landscape I live in so I call her every day, sometimes in the morning and sometimes late at night so she can hear the background noises of my neighborhood, the Campo dei Fiori, one of the busiest and noisiest places in all of Rome. So centrally located am I that my apartment windows and terrace are centered in the background of every postcard sold in Rome of the colorful Campo dei Fiori marketplace. Each morning at six, the vegetable, flower, and fish stalls are set up, followed by a complete two-hour cleaning each afternoon at two. Children play soccer in the square in the afternoon. Then the restaurants set up outdoor tables for the evening dinner crowd, followed by late evening concerts, fashion shows, or political demonstrations which end at midnight. At Vicki's end of the phone line, I hear sea lions barking in the background.

Against this constant barrage of noise from the Campo, I miss speaking to Vicki in person and hearing her movements around this apartment. I miss sharing with her the way being in Italy has changed the American routine of my life and the manner of my public language, a language now suffused with a few Italian phrases that I've memorized with great difficulty. It is true that, without her, I interact more with Italians on the street and my own knowledge of Italian increases daily. On the phone, Vicki tells me, "I miss you, I love you." When someone outside drags a shovel across the Roman cobblestones, Vicki asks what the noise is; by now I know without looking. I hear the fish peddler speaking on his cellular phone below my window in a different voice than the one he uses for selling. I'm beginning to recognize different makes of scooters by sound and I move quickly to the side of the street when I hear the Motoguzzi motorcycles of the *Carabinieri* come up behind me. There is no other motorcycle sound like it in all of Rome. Even those citizens who drive Motoguzzis don't drive their motorcycles like the *Carabinieri*. "I love you too," is what I always say in answer to Vicki.

I am told not to use Italian mail because I will probably return home before any mail arrives. But I like Italian mail. I'm too compulsive to use it, but I like the idea of slow Italian mail. There's nothing wrong with Italian mail, the world just changed and the system didn't. When I was in Italy the first time, every letter I sent via Italian mail arrived, sometimes in ten days and sometimes in three weeks. Now I would like to communicate *only* by Italian mail, but that pace of life is a luxury these days and *choosing* the slowest mail would be a political and personal act of self-determination. There's also something very romantic about writing a letter slowly over a period of days, then sending it and *waiting* for it to arrive at its destination.

I didn't understand the romance of slow mail until I found my father's letters to my mother dated from January 1944 to January 1947. They weren't married yet. He was twenty-seven in 1944 and my mother was twenty. They were separated for three years during and just after World War II. In those three years my mother lived in Tientsin, China, then moved to Shanghai, then back again to Tientsin; my father worked as an engineer in the unoccupied areas in the interior of China, designing and building bridges and roads, and he moved from city to city. The letters sometimes took one month to three months to arrive; sometimes my father would receive three of my mother's letters in one day, each one dated weeks apart.

Except for one letter from my mother, I only have my father's letters so the dialogue is one-sided. Most of the letters are written in Chinese and a few are written in English. What is remarkable about the letters is that my father rarely speaks (except in two letters) about the war, the Japanese, or the history of the moment. Instead, he engages my mother in conversations and asks questions, knowing full well that he probably won't get an answer for months. Sometimes he sends a second or third letter a few days later. They begin three or four dialogues in different letters, each one generated by the receipt of the last. Even more amazing, toward the end of 1946, when the strain of their separation is affecting their relationship, they argue and apologize in letters that again take a month or more to arrive. He becomes ill at one point and is hospitalized.

Again and again my father tells my mother how he loves her and admires her and that he is so much less of a person without her. My mother takes painting, piano, and ballet lessons in Shanghai. There's a tiny photo of my mother at twenty, leaning against the railing on a flight of stairs, tucked in among the pages. The natural light in the black and white photo makes her look completely at ease, content, happy, and luminously beautiful. She is wearing western clothes. My father encloses a photo of himself in another letter, standing on a bridge. It looks like twilight. He's wearing casual clothes with no jacket or tie. He is a very handsome man. You can even tell in the photo that he is tall for a Chinese, 6'2". Responding to a letter from my mother dated February 8, 1944 in which she said that he looked thin, he answers two and half months later on April 24 in an offended tone: "Who says I am thin? Look, my face is almost round. This photo was taken in the country where clothes are very casual and less bulky. I'm not wearing socks." He isn't wearing socks, as I find out in a later letter, not as a fashion statement, but because he can't find any that are big enough.

His letters are an interesting contrast in what he chooses to write about. In one letter dated February 7, 1944 he writes, "I am returning to North Fukien to build a bridge, a bridge I designed." This line is followed by, "A few days ago I had a beautiful dream. It seemed that I was in a theater in Tientsin. It was very crowded and I was looking for a place to sit. I saw you. We stared at each other without words." Later, when he is hospitalized, he tells my mother, "The true feeling of our love will touch everything. I am tearful with gratitude. I miss the person I love every day."

In letters written in English, he calls her "darling" or "dearest darling." His phrasing is different and more romantic. When he writes in English, the letters are more polished and constructed and he rarely includes any questions. On November 10, 1944 my father is still ill when he writes, "Darling, I love and admire you because of all of your beauty, your superior intelligence, your artistic talent, and your health. I look at your recent photo and cannot sleep. I am afraid of losing you because of our separation and my illness. I hesitate to tell you and not tell you my fear. However, to win your love by hiding my weakness would be to cover myself with falsehood, which is something I cannot redeem until I die. You are a perfect person." Then he tells my mother that the doctor says he has tuberculosis. "I was speechless," he writes. "When I left the doctor's office, I noticed that the leaves of the trees were very luxuriant in the autumn wind. After a rain, the air seemed more vital. I walked with my head down. I have not the heart to enjoy the beauty of nature. Life, death and separation are unavoidable. I do not have regret. I love you forever. I lift my head, stretch my arms, and assure you that I will continue to write until I cannot write any more."

He begins his treatments in the hospital. He writes on November 25 that the "boundaries of the day have disappeared." He must know that his letter of November 10 informing my mother of his tuberculosis has not arrived, yet he continues his conversation with her as if she knew the news, as if she had answered. "Life," he writes "is almost mechanical now. The slower your letters come, the more I long for your letters. I may lose all that I have hoped for with you. I will continue to honor you and honor the sparkling Saturday evening when we first met."

My father, Peter Hsu, recovered from tuberculosis and returned home from his three-year absence, and he and my mother, Maria Huang, were married in China. They left China to attend school in California; my father enrolled in graduate school in civil engineering at the University of California at Berkeley and my mother attended the California College of Arts and Crafts in Oakland. I was born in 1949 and they never returned to China. When I was seven, my father died at the age of forty from lung cancer and eight years later, three days before her fortieth birthday, my mother died. Since I am forty-eight, my only memories of them are as people younger than myself, and in most of my memories they are in their early thirties. When I was much younger, I used to measure my life against their lives at that age as if we were contemporaries. After I passed forty and lost their ages as reference points, their lives transfigured into symbols— of youth, of happiness, of commitment, of love, but the problem with symbols is their silent meaning.

When I found these letters, it gave me back the twenty-seven-year-old voice of my father. Can I express my love to Vicki as completely as my father expressed his love to my mother, or have I learned to love in silence? I should be able to find my voice; I'm a writer.

But, in our hectic and busy lives, I tell her on the phone, "I love you, too," and go on to the next topic.

My father writes on January 4, 1945 that by the time his letter arrives in my mother's hands it will be springtime where she is and that when she answers it will be summer where he is and another season will have emerged before he can reply. He writes that he has started a diary because of the inability to communicate more quickly. In it, he writes, "I feel a strange and unspeakable depression in my heart."

On February 28, 1945, my father notes that he is leaving the hospital. His mood changes: "Yesterday was January 15, according to the lunar calendar. Day suddenly cleared up after being cloudy for more than two months. I was in bed resting when the noon light passed through the green leaves of the trees by my window, and the shadows danced in a slight breeze on my white sheets. It was so beautiful I could not sleep. In the evening the moon illuminated the fog against the mountain peaks. I thought of you and home. You are the best companion on a journey. When I am alone at night, I think of our laughter. I pick up this pen and talk to you." My father is in and out of the hospital and continues to work when he is out of the hospital for four hours at a time. He manages to win a monetary award by figuring out a formula to build bridges and roads with the wartime shortage of materials. He rereads my mother's letters to him. She returns to Tientsin from Shanghai. By April he is getting stronger and even able to play basketball. His engineering team beats the other team 55 to 5 and they win a trophy. "I was the best," he boasts. "In the basketball game I wore the dancing shoes, the same shoes I danced in when we danced the waltz at the Peking Hotel. They were the most elegant shoes I had, but now they are no longer so. They have been repaired twice and patched. They have more wrinkles than my face after a long journey. I would have thrown them away long ago if they were not so historically important." He speaks of walking in the snow with my mother while wearing those same shoes. They warmed themselves by a fire; she peeled the layers of her clothes off until she wore only a backless blouse. "Your back was cold, my feet were numb."

In May of 1945 my father travels to a town close enough to Shanghai for them to attempt to meet; they discuss their plans, but the mail takes so long that the moment passes. My father remarks that her letter dated March 1, 1945 took three months and thirteen days to reach him. In it my mother speaks of the poor weather in Tientsin where it is cold, then suddenly hot. By the time he receives the letter, it is summer where he is and they've been apart for a year and a half. In July, he writes about his recovery: he has gained weight, goes swimming, and has a tan. One letter is only eight lines long.

Vicki calls me in Rome and tells me there were two small earthquakes in Seattle.

On September 5, 1945, my father mentions that once the road-building work in Min Pei is done, he can go home. He finally mentions the war and writes about the difficulty of building bridges with a shortage of material and equipment. He is inspired to continue by the sight of American planes flying overhead. Five days later he receives a two-month-old letter from my mother dated July 9. He is uncertain about the mood and tone in her letter and notes that she is meeting new friends he has never heard of. At the end of his short reply, he writes, "How is the family? I stop here. Victory of the War of Resistance."

On November 13, 1945 he worries about not receiving a letter from his own family in six months, but my mother is able to communicate to him that they are well. Japanese soldiers in Peiping and Tientsin have surrendered and the two cities have regained their freedom and security. "We should celebrate," he writes. He talks of building the highway for the last ten months and how many of his friends have scattered in different directions after the war. "The difficult and hard time is over. What we have suffered in the past eight years causes me to tremble every time I think about it."

On December 6, he notes that my mother's last letter arrived in twenty days. "Very fast," he writes. He writes about traveling to meet her soon, but hasn't written anything about being in love with my mother in months. On January 5, 1946, he says that his work is almost done, but the railroad from Shanghai to Tientsin is still damaged; a ship from Fuchow to Shanghai is possible, but one was sunk recently when it hit a mine; and he doesn't have enough money to travel by plane. He asks my mother if she has any better information about getting home.

Now, people are getting married. My mother and my father are meeting new friends at parties that only one of them attends. He goes to the opera for the first time and, on another occasion, sees the movie *Arsenic and Old Lace*. He knows of a man who is going to Tientsin, so my father buys a pair of silk stockings for him to take to my mother. Letters arrive more quickly, but the roads and railroad are still unusable and mines are still floating in the water off the coast. My father is fully recovered by now, but since he is unable to travel to Tientsin, he takes on another job, which further delays his return. Both my father and mother are slightly jealous of the other's new life and new friends in the post–World War II days. My father writes to my mother in English on February 1946:

Dearest Darling,
Having read your letter of Jan. 8, my mind is rather mixed. My thoughts always follow your words which you told me in your last letter. I don't know how to handle this if you really feel that way. I don't know even how the world seems to me if I lost you. Darling, don't think that way. It is no good for the both of us.
    After I read your letter, I went out to take a walk. I

thought the cold air would do a little good for me. I stag-
gered along the stone paved road. I did not know which
direction I should go. I just followed a man whose name I
did not know. I walked through the crowded streets. The
darkness. I went into a restaurant finally. I drank a bottle
of wine. I am not a good drinker. A bottle of wine is too
much for me. All I wanted was to forget the present moment. Yes, it really did it. The earth went around before
my eyes. I could feel it. I saw Jupiter.

Since it now only takes two to three weeks for a letter to arrive,
they argue by mail. Then suddenly, without notice, letters take longer,
sometimes even months. In April the mail system recovers and on
April 13, 1946, my father writes, "I feel very sad after I read your
letter of April 9th. You sounded very sour. I do not know how I
offended you. After reading your letter my heart is frozen. Letters
take so long to arrive sometimes. If one word is misplaced, it is
dangerous." Eleven days later he writes again, in English:

Dearest Darling,
I love you, darling. I love you. Do you hear? I love you
more than anything in the world. What makes you think I
have changed? Oh, darling, not me. And, I am sure (100%)
that you love me too. I have no doubt about that. Having
been away for three years, I have had no other girl friend,
not a single one. The war separated you and me for so long.
There is a misunderstanding between us. I should make it
clear once and for all. It was not my wish to leave you. I
hate the war, because it separated us.
  Everyone I know, knows that I am going to marry you.
I will not go anywhere unless you are by my side.

"Love makes time pass.
Time makes love pass."

That is wrong. It cannot be applied to our situation. Time makes our love more intense. Just try to think of the very moment when I will be facing you and I am able to see the face that time separated from me. The face that could only be seen in dreams, can now be touched. I can kiss it. My dreams come true. For years I have stretched my hands and tried to hold you in my hands, but it was impossible. Darling, I miss you.

I wish I could ask my father why he choose to write in English at such an important moment. Perhaps, it was to make my mother read more slowly and work harder at understanding a language neither one of them were born to. Among the pile of letters, I found a short story, written in English, that my father sent to my mother, in which he imagines their married life.

The Great Waltz

"Everything seems to be all right. What time is it dear?" she asked. There was no reply. She started to whistle "The Tale of the Vienna Woods" without waiting for an answer. She was busy cooking in the kitchen.

"Boy! What a woman!" he said. She was startled by his answer. She turned around to find out what was wrong with him. He was sitting at ease in the kitchen by the window, his feet up on a chair, and he was eating cookies and candies, concentrating his attention on *Film Fun* magazine.

"What are you looking at? Let me see. You haven't answered my question yet." She looked over his shoulder at the pictures in *Film Fun,* but it was not an interesting picture for a woman.

It was early September 1947. The newly married couple lived in a small apartment. Tonight, they were expecting their friends, Jessie, Joan, Norma, and her fiancé for dinner. She was busy all day, decorating the windows with new curtains she had painted herself. She moved the chairs and sofa so that everyone could sit close to each other. She polished the brass teapot. She pushed her piano back toward the stand lamp to make the room more cozy. She put a black stone that looked like a man on the mantel of the fireplace. She liked it very much, but her husband said it was silly to put on the fireplace mantel, because the fireplace was the center of activity. Both of them wanted to decorate it with their favorite piece.

Since he was an engineer, she let him fix the lamps in the living room so that the light would reflect off the ceiling and walls. The bulbs were properly sheltered, the illumination was moderate.

"Darling, go take a bath before they come. Wash your fingernails carefully. I don't mind if you use some of my 'Soir de Paris.' I just don't want the smell of gasoline in the room tonight."

He was a successful engineer and he liked his job. Every day he drove his car to his office and came back home at 5:30 after a day's hard work. He always came home with a dirty face and hands and oil stains on his clothes. After work he usually sank down into the sofa with his work clothes on. He would listen to the radio and eat a piece of pie. Tonight, the air in the room was tingling with the smell of gasoline and perfume. She did not like his gasoline, but he liked her perfume.

After their dinner, and everyone was relaxing in the living room, eating dessert, he said to her, "Let me have a piece of your cake if you don't want any more." His large figure must have had a large stomach because his appetite was awfully fine. He knew that his guests would not laugh at him for asking for an extra share, because they were old classmates. They had all grown up now, but they never forgot those happy days of school life. When they got together, they laughed and talked just like the old days. Every Saturday or on holidays, they got together. They talked about the past, their hopes, the happy events, and sometimes they danced if the music on the radio was especially fine. They were young and their lives seemed like flowers in May.

"You have completely changed," Jessie said to the hostess, sitting before the piano.

"Yes, she has, just look at the hair, lips, eyelashes, especially the figure. Marriage is good for you," Joan said.

Jessie danced her fingers over the keys. Norma said to Jessie, "Play something."

"Oh, no, let our hostess play something! After all it's her piano and she is going to have a concert next Sunday night," Jessie said in a loud voice.

The newly married couple eyed each other for a moment and then she sat down at the piano and began to play selections from "The Great Waltz." It was a happy tune and he sank back down into the sofa with his pipe in his hand. The curling smoke made his mind swim in reveries. He remembered when he first took his bride out. They went ice skating. Her beauty and charm thrilled him. He remembered calling on her with her permission. It was just before he was to leave on a special job and he asked her whether he could have a date with her the next Sunday before he said good-bye. Her answer was not favorable. Time got fast when they were together.

I think my father would've liked the fact that I became a writer, combining what he attempted in these letters with my mother's artistic talents.

My mother's only letter in the pile of letters is dated September 10, 1946 and it is written in English and addressed to her friend Jessie. She refers to my father as "Mr. Hsu":

Jessie,
I have received your letter some days ago. I forgot if I have told you that Mr. Hsu and I were engaged on August 15th. I am working now and am very busy. According to the lunar calendar it is August 15th and it should be a holiday, but we don't have a vacation. My job is taking care of English letters, receiving them and answering them and to give out certificates of immunization. It is very interesting. I've been here for a week, substituting for Miss Kao who went to Shanghai. When she comes back, I will be unemployed.

How are you? Are you working? In your letter, you mentioned your recent situation. Are you really divorced from Mr. Tseng? That is regrettable. If you have divorced, I hope you do not take it to heart. What a heartbreaking thing. I hope you take care of yourself.

I am enclosing a letter for Mr. Hsu, please hand to him. Thank you. Hope you will write soon.

Maria

In my father's last letter, dated October 29, 1946, he tells my mother that he was able to book passage on a ship, but the sailing date was postponed indefinitely. His return is uncertain. He asks my mother to continue to write. He muses about going to graduate school in California, about the two of them returning to rebuild China and about raising a family there. I understand from my aunt Ching-yi, my father's sister (who translated the letters), that he returned at the end of 1946, after a three-year absence. My father and mother were married in September 1947, sailed to San Francisco in 1948, and settled in Berkeley, where my father began his graduate studies. The Communists took over China in 1949 and I was born in the same year. They never returned home. My father is buried in Oakland, California and my mother is buried in Los Angeles. Both of their graves face west, toward the ocean.

When I visit the Santi Quattro Coronati in Rome, the church is being cleaned. I ring a bell by a side door and ask the nun if I can visit the cloister in the adjoining convent. I am immediately struck by the peaceful, simple beauty of this place, lined as it is by small arches and petite columns. At the center of the cloister is a courtyard and a small garden with a round marble fountain engraved with the faces of lions who seem almost to be smiling. The water cascades over the side of the fountain into an octagonal pool where goldfish swim. Someone has thrown white flowers in the pool. The light is completely different on each of the four sides of the tiny courtyard. The nun is seated at one corner and is speaking with a man and his daughter, who looks to be six or seven. She is dressed in a pink dress with white lace, white socks, and patent-leather Mary Janes. She smiles as the nun speaks to her. I think this little courtyard is the most peaceful place in all of Rome.

When I re-enter the church, two men have decorated it with hundreds of white roses in terra cotta pots in preparation for a wedding. A violinist is tuning his violin to the church organ. He and the organist begin playing together and the small church is filled with music that brings the thirteenth-century interior alive. The effect of the music and the white roses in the church is utterly romantic. In the natural light from the windows, I begin writing a letter home which I will send by Italian mail. I will return home before it arrives. In my letter to Vicki, I explain how much I love her. I borrow my father's voice in some sentences, even though I'm much older.

BEULAH LAND

CAROLYN SEE

MY DAUGHTER CLARA had shut herself up in her room. This wasn't an adolescent tantrum; it was worse, far worse. She lay on her back, tears pooling in her ears. "I've got tears in my ears from lying on my back, crying over you," I suggested, but she was so far gone she couldn't laugh, or cry harder, or even give me the scornful look I deserved. Her sister Lisa, who must have been about twenty-five at the time and living at home for a while, stood beside me. We looked down at Clara, whose features had thickened with grief. There was really nothing we could do, or say. Clara's father—one of those divorce-fathers who hang around just enough to enkindle an enormous semi-requited love in their offspring—had decided to make a new life for himself and was hauling off to Oregon. That meant instead of seeing him once a week or once a month, Clara would see him twice a year. If he remembered, if he felt like it.

Not that he wasn't entitled to go, poor guy. We all get to figure out how to put together a new life. But it didn't help matters that he had a new wife and a new kid and that by way of that kid he'd indignantly fended off one of my recent requests for child support by saying, "I hardly have enough to take care of my *real* family!" Oh, horrors. Oh, sadness. Oh, the terror of being abandoned, and not sufficiently loved.

Lisa was Clara's half-sister; I'd married not just one (in my eyes) bozo, but two, and Lisa's father kept slithering away, not in the straightforward "I'm going to Oregon" fashion, but more like "You're selling out, you probably are a racist, you're the kind of bourgeois girl who wants a front *lawn* when she grows up!" Thus he peppered his daughter with snippy remarks and curled lips and Eurasian snickers and went for months at a time without calling her. (Until she got a clue—and went for two straight years without calling him.)

There's something about a family that wants to fly apart, and that centrifugal force is powered by something that's the opposite of love. On the other hand, there's something about a family that wants to stay together—that's why Lisa came home, after a few years of high adventure in Greece and other places; it's possible that centripetal force, that force toward continuity, might be powered by apathy or inertia or torpor or even the compulsion to hang around and pay off a few grudges, but there's also a strong possibility that it's powered by love.

Lisa and I gave up on Clara and went downstairs to watch television. It was too much, really; it was too sad. Lisa had been missing her father, mourning him, waiting for his calls, since she was three, and kicking back a generation, my own father had decided to flee the scene when I was eleven. "It was too much for me," he explained later. "I knew that if I stayed around, I'd go mad." Well, I could get behind what he was saying; I knew my mother as well as he did, but I never did get the nerve to ask him, "What about me? You just left me there so that I could go mad instead?" No, I smiled, and waited for his phone calls, and plain adored him, and suffered the tortures of the damned when he decided that the mature thing for him to do was to haul down to Tampa, Florida, and sink all his friends' money into the frozen shrimp business.

Ah, well. Water under the bridge. Lisa and I focused on the television and after about ten minutes it became clear to us that we had to be looking at the worst miniseries ever made. (There is no hyperbole in this statement. We've seen them all and we have a high tolerance for bad television, but this was transcendent; this was amazing; this was *Beulah Land* with Leslie Ann Warren [I *think* it was Leslie Ann Warren; I know it was the worst, the very worst ...])

We got up and went upstairs to Clara. "Honey, we know you feel awful but there's something amazing on television ..." She didn't move or stir.

We went downstairs and watched some more and went back up and pried Clara up to a sitting position. As I remember, Lisa said something sisterly about how she might as well feel bad sitting up as lying down, and we got on each side of her and more or less dragged her down to the couch in the living room. Maybe every family has its Beth (as in Meg, Jo, Beth, and Amy), the vulnerable one, the one to whom bad things shouldn't happen, and that night, at least, Clara was our Beth (although when it had happened to defenseless Lisa she was Beth, and back when I was eleven, God damn it, and hadn't done anyone any real harm in my life, I was Beth.)

We sat Clara down between us and watched the most disorganized southern family in Christendom go steadily down the drain. For one thing, they kept misplacing their accents and then getting them back again with a vengeance; for another, a white overseer had some bad designs on them. I don't know, it was bad, but was it bad enough? Clara was encased in pain; her life, all that she loved in her life had been smashed to smithereens. Her father (it seemed) didn't care about her, she was left in a house full of losers; she was left.

Then someone on television got extremely indignant at the villain: "You killed my mammy! You killed my pappy! And you split my lip!" Lisa and I went into hysterics, and Clara—her face, I remember, thick and swollen from crying, her cheeks glistening with tears—had to laugh. She went right back to crying again. But I was moved to utter what has become an article of faith with me, and beyond just "believing" it I have reason by now to believe that it really is true: "Listen, he only *thinks* he's going somewhere. He'll be back. They always come back. You can't get rid of them. They're always around." *Damn straight,* Lisa may or may not have echoed at that point. Who knew if it was true? It certainly seemed like it should be true.

Because if there's a force that scatters, there's a force that reassembles. Think of Ulysses. Then think of Penelope.

FLASH FORWARD A few years. I'm doing a magazine piece on a group called L.A.D.I.E.S., or "Life After Divorce Is Eventually Sane." This is made up of the ex-wives of Michael Landon and Buddy Ebsen and Jerry Lewis and even Herve what's-his-name (de plane! de plane! de vorce!). These ladies, having been dumped, had to suffer double humiliations; it was bad enough being dumped, God knows, but to have to read about it in the tabloids was awful. So these women had thought up all kinds of brave coping devices and I was doing a piece about them for *McCall's.*

But one lady didn't seem to get the overall picture. She might not have been to enough meetings. "I don't care what he's done, I don't care who he's with now. I just want him back. He's my king. I love him. Oh, he's so kingly!"

"So . . . you're committed to the idea of not being a victim in the relationship?"

"I pray for him to come back every day. My life isn't worth living without him. I pray for him twice a day, in the morning and at night before I sleep."

"So you won't have any resentments, is that it?"

"No! I pray for him to come *back* to me, because we belong together. I went out and bought a beautiful new Bible with a white cover and I had his name engraved on it and that Bible stays in bed beside me on his pillow, where he'll find it when he comes back, because I *know* the Lord is sending him back to me, sooner rather than later!"

She was a pretty little blonde, quite tearstained, very determined. I kept seeing her on religious cable TV, where she'd have her head bowed in earnest prayer, and a slew of dubious looking ministers and ministers' helpers would be praying along for this bozo (from a bad but famous sitcom) to come home to his wife who loved him— praying not because he was sinful, or even the least bit misguided, but because she loved him; he was her king. She wanted him back in that bed with her, with that big white Bible right across his rib cage.

And what do you know? He came back. Because you could do a lot worse than stay with a cute blonde who goes on every public venue she can think of to say you're her king. (And there's no point in crossing God either, unless there's a pretty good reason for it.)

So. It's a form of Tai Chi, isn't it? People scrambling off and saying, OK, that's it, I'm out of here, I can't take it any longer, if I don't get some room to live my own life, I'll full-out tumble right over and perish. And the person who's *left* is left with the perplexing notion of how to respond. Because when you're abandoned it's as though they've pushed you off into that existential abyss, you're in free fall, and it's very hard to *think* when you're in free fall. You can't blame the person who's falling for going into terminal aaaaaiiiiieeeee! and keeping that up for the rest of his or her natural life.

The person who's leaving is often not only leaving *you*, but his mother (or her father) or taking some other arcane revenge on some-body whose name you didn't catch, so that's another reason why the person who's being abandoned feels so *abandoned*, so bummed, so done-wrong-by. (My mother, when my father left, went into hysterics and stayed that way for close to twenty years, all the way up into and beyond another marriage.) When you're in free fall it's hard to get your bearings. When somebody leaves he's making a statement that goes far beyond the personal: It's like (a) I can't stand you anymore, and (b) there isn't any redeeming social value in these human connections. I want to disconnect so badly that I'm willing to sell all my human colleagues in this "connection" enterprise down the river! Or (c) if that isn't plain enough for you, I don't *love* you anymore. The Velcro of love on your shirt doesn't stick anymore! That's why you're falling in that abyss, *get it?*

Except, except. The earth is spinning even as I write this, even as you read it. The planet itself is in some kind of fall, and so are we all. It's possible, by an effort of will, to gaze around from a "falling" position and say, "Well, *I'm still and stable*, I'm at the center of things, and some of the people around me seem to be slipping and sliding away, the poor things! It's too bad, but I'm taking the position that they aren't going anywhere, nobody's going anywhere, because centripetal force is stronger than centrifugal force, and that's what—for these few days, years, decades, I'm going to be defining as love. People don't leave because they can't. There is no leaving, get it? We're all humans linked to the human condition, and our connections are stronger than our separations."

About forty years ago, Simone de Beauvoir came to America and had an affair with Nelson Algren. The lady must have been desperate for a good time after all that existentialism and the rigors of World War II. She came to Chicago and drank whiskey and listened to jazz and went to backyard barbecues, and she lay down with Nelson on his monklike cot—because, remember? he just wanted to live in his furnished room and write great literature and not sell out. It was soon over, and he dismissed it as "a routine love affair."

Routine! Oh, the horror! And he said it in print and in interviews, so that all her friends could read it and hear about it, not to mention Jean-Paul Sartre, who was fooling around with that toothsome Juliette Greco at the time! Oh, the horror of being dumped and disavowed and discounted! And unloved.

Except that Simone de Beauvoir took another whole position. It had been an earthshaking love affair. It had provided physical, mental, spiritual, emotional energy quite unlike any other love affair in the Western World up to this time. Antony and Cleopatra were bargain-basement, small-change chumps compared to Simone and Nelson on that little cot with the ratty army blanket in that Chicago furnished room. What was it the metaphysical poet had said? "One little room an everywhere?" He got *that* right, Simone said. And Simone and Nelson were the ones in that fabled little room.

And Nelson, probably as mean-spirited as the next unprincipled Yahoo, certainly dead set against "commitment" and attachment and lawns and houses and the whole heterosexual march of time, must have felt a tremor, in the pit of his stomach, the back of his knees. He'd pushed Simone over into the abyss, but *he* seemed to be the one who was falling. The woman's *nuts*, he cried! She's out of her gourd! Because it was just routine! *Routine!*

Oh, that Algren, she mused, but not to him. Oh, the days and nights we had together. Quite astonishing. An intensity that no modern language—certainly not French or English—can begin to express.

"Routine," Nelson Algren protested weakly. But who was he, just some joker on a cot some place. She was the Queen of Existentialism; she was going to be buried in a great big tomb in a French cemetery right next to Sartre with bouquets of flowers brought every day by devotees. Nelson hadn't understood something. If someone was going to get disconnected, and *if* it involved an abyss, she was staying safe on the canyon's ledge and the other person would be going into free fall.

If not, she had a thousand filaments, a thousand varieties of Velcro (I know, it hadn't been invented yet!) a thousand little jars of Krazy Glue, so if he decided to stick (around) he was certainly more than welcome.

And in Nelson's later writing, after he got over his tantrums, he began referring again to that headstrong philosopher in another whole tone: She wore those crazy turbans! She loved to ride those bikes! She had that outrageous French accent! And a great pair of legs. He gave in to a centripetal force far stronger than his cheap desire to denigrate, debase, devaluate, and just plain flee. He found himself connected, a prisoner of love, and the more he struggled to release himself the more glued on he became.

"I always try to speak of your father with such kindness and affection that people think he's dead," my first stepmother told me. "And if you ever get a divorce, Carolyn, I suggest you do the same."

Seen in this way, "love" doesn't become the stuff of poets, or even, necessarily, an agreement between two people. It's a *position:* He's not going anywhere. He only *thinks* he's going somewhere! He'll always be around.

Now I have to say that I myself have not always adhered to this position (although I stuck so close to my own dad that I ended up being lifelong friends with two of my stepmothers and one of his girlfriends—up in her eighties now, utterly elegant with her Worth perfume and her Chanel suits). But when it came to those two husbands of my youth, I came down squarely on the fence. To be frank, I found them sadly wanting, too damn crabby, hard to please, un-ambitious, too fond of drugs, and drink, and other ladies. Wasn't it easier to label them assholes and groan on at length about being left—all pitiful and unloved?

But had *I* not been just a little too damn crabby, hard to please, ambitious to a fault, too fond of drugs, drink, and (even) other men? Not to mention crying fits and sulking matches and wasted after-noons and evenings watching bad TV? (How come *Beulah Land* hap-pened to be on in our house in the first place?) And weren't both those guys pretty funny, and didn't they sometimes run through the house with water pistols, and didn't they fall down laughing and didn't they both like to travel and didn't they both have full steamer trunks of bright ideas and original theories that they didn't mind sharing? And most of all, weren't both of them genetically 50 percent responsible for two of the most amazing, charming and out-and-out *good* young women I'd ever met in my life? So that whenever I did say to either Lisa or Clara, "You're mighty like your dad," it was always the most respectful compliment, because they took the sweetest, dearest characteristics of their dads and distilled them into what was best about being human.

So I didn't want to say that they were the greatest guys on earth; I wouldn't (God forbid!) want to pray them back into my bed with the aid of a big white Bible. I wanted the freedom to call them both assholes and to roll around the house and cry (well, not for *too* long, since I soon found my real life's companion and he took a fairly dim view of that sort of thing), but what I really wanted was for those guys not to go anywhere far away.

I wanted them to be part of our family. And I wanted to be part of theirs.

This is, then, an interim report on the power of centripetal force, how a set of females took the position that—free fall or not—there is a *glue*, made up of good manners, relentless sociability, the utter refusal to be "abandoned," and the zen-insistence that not only are all of us still friends, we are all part of one big happy—if over-extended—family.

So that during the last thirty years, one of my ex-mothers-in-law has come up to me at least a dozen times and whispered, "Carolyn, you always were my favorite," and I can only answer, "Oh, I bet you say that to all his girls." And such was the level of welcome in the other family (not right away, but eventually, as the dust settled), that my other ex-mother-in-law gestured expansively for my dear friend John to come over and sit by her at one of the big parties we all seem to show up at, "Because, after all, John, we're family."

Because it's easier to sink back into the center than keep on heading out.

Because "out there" is only the monastery, or the brothel in Thailand, or the Montana furnished room.

Because those two daughters I know fastened themselves to their dads like ticks and would not be dislodged, would not.

Because those two dads finally succumbed to the notion that they weren't going anywhere, that even if they went to Mississippi or Oregon or Finland or India or went waltzing off all the way around the world, they'd still land back here, because they had family here, and that's just the way it was.

FLASH FORWARD TO the present. My daughters and I are currently involved in a very small project in Santa Monica, an outreach program for homeless, mentally ill women. Clara discovered Daybreak while doing field work for an undergraduate class in feminism at UCLA. She found a "shelter" down by the beach: a place where two homeless women could spend the night, each in her own cubicle, for up to ninety days, and if they could succeed in getting it together, they might luck out and get their own affordable apartments, out of free fall and out once again on the lip of dry land.

Besides the shelter, Daybreak operated a "drop in" center, where women who couldn't bear to spend a night under an enclosing roof could stay out in the streets at night, but drop in during the day, take a hot shower, have a hot meal, play some cards or checkers, or rest, or chat, and go "shopping" for a clean set of clothes. These women were pretty far up on the crazy charts, and yet—they had all come from somewhere, all come from families. Some of them had children who'd gotten sick of the whole process; a good many of them had husbands who'd drifted off without sufficiently clueing them in on how to make the car payment or take care of property taxes. Now they were true bag ladies, disoriented, filthy, unlovable, unloved. All of them had parents. Most of them, especially the young ones, had been hideously abused. Not only raped! They'd been thrown through plate glass windows, right from the living room out onto the lawn, so that all the neighbors could see how much they were not loved. Another dad took it upon himself to bean his little girl with a large sack of sand—a theatrical weight—when she was on stage during a recital. She took the hint and hit the road.

No wonder they were crazy, Clara felt, and went to work with them, trying, one by one, to right the thousand wrongs she saw each day. Lisa and I ended up on the Resource Board with maybe twenty other women of good intentions. The story behind the fundraising was this: These women could be any of us, we could be any of these women, according to the luck of the draw, a couple of missed paychecks, and the rearrangement of a few brain chemicals.

Some women on the Board believed this—I know I did—and some didn't. Some women clung strongly to the position that their education and good hearts and good grooming and good intentions would save them from the street; that even if their brains did do a 180-degree turn one day, they'd have somebody there to drive them over to the Neuro-psychiatric Institute at UCLA where they'd get bombarded with the right medication until they'd be bright as new pennies again.

But there were times when that mock-up of reality shivered and shook. Someone on the staff killed herself. That shouldn't have happened; she was on the staff. A beautiful woman on the Resource Board got a nasty surprise when her husband left her. And another one. And another one. Some women took it fairly well, but one was fully heartbroken. Here was the story; any one of us could be any one of them. Enough anguish, enough rejection, enough pain, could actually rearrange your chemicals, might that not be true? And when you start to fall, if there's no one there to catch you or hold you or prop you up, well, we all know what can happen next.

This is not a digression! Far from it. Every year the Daybreak Board holds a fundraiser. It's a small one, and in the Greater Los Angeles scheme of things it's positively minuscule. But here it was, coming up again, about 300 people showing up for brunch in a tiny air museum with little planes taking off outside and little fossil planes from the twenties inside, and over on the side a silent auction, put together in great part by Clara—who at the beginning of this essay we saw as a sixteen-year-old, flat on her back poleaxed by grief, tears in her ears, loveless and alone, except for two females who propped her up and made her watch that terribly bad actor: "You killed my mammy! You killed my pappy! And you split my lip!" Now she browsed among the coupons for free yoga lessons and dinners at Japanese restaurants, serene and flowery, in flowing skirts and a wide straw hat. Her husband, a nice guy who doesn't seem to have fleeing on his mind, was with her.

Some wonderful black jazz musicians began to play, and next to me a woman who'd been left by her husband began to weep. "Oh, Carolyn, he left me, after thirty years! I'll never get over it, never! I'm alone now, all alone."

She was a sweet woman, and so pretty. I wanted to say: Look! He's as alone as you are. Or, Come on, you still have your kids. Or, Whatever happens, we're all alive now in this big airy room, and outside little planes are taking off into the morning sky. But she didn't have any strings attached to her; there wasn't any force field accruing around her; she was in free fall.

I'd been thinking about what I was going to write for this anthology—hadn't everything on earth already been written about love? I left the silent auction and went back to the table that the family had taken over; my sweet friend, John, and a friend of his, and Clara and her husband, and Lisa and her husband and her two sons. Nobody looked like they were going anywhere. Of course, you never know. But if one of us skidded out the rest of us would still be there (and those two dads, still squirming and wiggling just a bit, staying in regular contact with their daughters, who'd seen to it.)

There was a little breath of calm. In the way that art helps life along sometimes, a beautiful black guy began to sing, "... too weak to break the chains that bind me, I need no shackles to remind me, I'm just a prisoner of love." Yeah, that's it, I thought. It's a lot harder to leave than it is to stay. Nobody's going anywhere at this table, and that's all there is to it.

We did good deeds for homeless women, stuck down hard to white folding chairs by centripetal force, by the tenacious Velcro of love.

THE LOVE INTEREST

ELIZABETH McCRACKEN

BECAUSE I AM the child of a happy marriage, I had to learn about love from Abbott and Costello. While my friends were listening to Shaun Cassidy and Jimmy McNicol and other mid-seventies puppyish sandy-haired younger-brother heartthrobs, I was studying two long-dead middle-aged men in gray suits. My friends would never have understood, even if I had tried to explain. Abbott and Costello weren't handsome, they were old, they didn't sing, they wore suits. Maybe Bud Abbott was dapper, in a con-man way, but Lou Costello was fat and sloppy and childish, a hopeful patsy. Not exactly the kind of men to make a prepubescent schoolgirl swoon, and possibly that's why I liked them: no other girl would. Every Saturday, I watched another one of their movies, which a local station showed under the grand title *Abbott and Costello Theater.* I did not know all the words to the "Shadow Dancing" or "Staying Alive," but I had memorized "Who's On First," "The Mustard Sketch," and "Jonah and the Whale," burlesque comedy routines already ancient when Abbott and Costello filmed them in the 1940s.

At the start of every movie, there they were, the couple in question. The boys joined the army, then the navy. They met Franken-

189

stein, Boris Karloff, the Keystone Kops. They investigated dude ranches and haunted houses. And while they were doing all of this, they argued terribly, about the same things, sometimes violently. You couldn't look into Bud and Lou's hearts and understand why they were married, they just were, they just would be forever. Really, it was hard to figure out what they saw in each other. They were always going to break each other's hearts. What made them think this was a good idea?

What *could* explain Abbott and Costello except love?

They were two people who so completely belonged together you couldn't imagine them apart. When one was on the screen without the other, he looked lost. I mean, they loved each other, obviously they loved each other, they were inseparable in name and in fact. Even so, in a lot of Abbott and Costello movies, the screenwriters added a subplot: The Love Interest, a blandly good-looking man and woman who didn't much like each other at the start but were sure to kiss by the end. The Love Interest always had the same premise: the idea of love is raised; love is threatened; finally and at the last minute love triumphs and the credits come up. Sometimes the Andrews Sisters sing; sometimes Lou Costello whistles, badly, a tender comment, not at all hubba-hubbaish. I can hear my grandmother ask, *Is this love, that can be put in so much peril by so little?* Surely not.

Surely this is love: *Abbott and Costello Theater*, every Saturday, a Boy-Has-Boy-Repeat-to-End-Repeat-Next-Week Story. That's the kind of love story *I'm* interested in, an endless series of black and white movies or TV shows, where love and partnership are a foregone conclusion. Laurel and Hardy, Abbott and Costello, Burns and Allen: they are together, they will be together, their bodies may be threatened (by pianos, by cream pies, by angry landlords with big black mustaches) but their relationship never is. They get mad at each other, but at the end of the movie—iris out—two people will be left, walking across the movie lot to begin the next adventure. A kiss and weepy embrace are all very well and good, but in real life that's not the end of the story. It's barely the start.

The Love Interest bored me silly. Who needs an extra, sugar-sweet man-woman couple? It's hard to keep good-looking black-and-white people straight. I always knew Abbott and Costello. Though I was a kid and therefore liked silly, aimless Lou Costello best, I understood that he wouldn't have been nearly so funny without Bud Abbott there, angrily saying, "Talk sense." A good straight man makes his comic funnier by telling him not to act so funny; he makes the comic human by reminding him of the ways of the world. The comic makes the straight man human with goofy sweetness. They improve each other. That, too, is a love story.

It's probably worth admitting that I am a child of one tall blonde shy person and one short brunette extrovert. I'm not saying my parents remind me in most ways of Abbott and Costello—I have never seen my mother do a spit take; my father isn't always trying to double-talk his wife out of a sawbuck—but it can't be denied: as a couple, they're a sight gag. Anyone would describe them this way: a great big guy and a little tiny woman. They even have props: my father has a thick white beard; my mother wears her hair in a bun and walks with two canes. Ambling down the street, they are as recognizable as any comedy team. You can spot the McCrackens a mile away, same as Abbott and Costello, same as Chaplin.

I am old enough now to regard my friends' marriages as entertainment. My favorite real life couples are comedy teams: one dreamer, one pragmatist. One social creature, one indulgent homebody. There's nothing I like so well as watching two people wittily and fondly bumping heads. There are couples of whom it is said, "It's as if they share one soul." Do the math—one soul between two people is not enough. Give me a couple with a good routine: the pancake story, the day we got married, our cross-country car trip with both dogs and both cats and one sleeping bag. It's what I look for in any pal: I want to feel funnier with them than without them. Vaudeville and burlesque are dead. We only have each other to pick up the slack.

WHAT REALLY SOLD me on Abbott and Costello was *The Abbott and Costello Book* by Jim Mullholland, one of the most important books of childhood. It taught me the pleasures of research: suddenly, having read it, I was the foremost expert on Abbott and Costello in the neighborhood, maybe even in all of Newton, Massachusetts, certainly in Miss Capuzzo's fifth grade class. I knew the titles and plotlines of their movies, which studios produced them, the names of their children. The book told me to keep an eye out for secret things in their movies: William Frawley, later Fred Mertz in *I Love Lucy*, as a blustery bad guy in *One Night in the Tropics*, Abbott and Costello's first movie; a teenaged Ella Fitzgerald in *Ride 'Em, Cowboy*, her movie debut, singing "A Tisket, A Tasket." Look, there's one of the Three Stooges dressed in sailor's whites; there's Margaret Dumont, cheating on the Marx Brothers and getting what she deserves.

Comedians' off-screen lives are famously unfunny, but I had never heard that before *The Abbott and Costello Book*. Previously I'd read about how tragedy was something you triumphed over, almost a good thing, a requirement for future greatness. Annie Sullivan's eyesight failed, which made it possible for her to meet and teach Helen Keller; Helen Keller was blind and deaf and mute and angry, which made it possible for her to meet Annie Sullivan, who taught her to communicate with the world, which made them both wonderful and miraculous people, worthy of book reports and filmstrips. Hardship in the books of my youth was instructive, both for those who suffered and those who read.

But Lou Costello suffered from rheumatic heart disease and had to take a year off from his radio show. The day he was scheduled to come back, his son, Lou Jr., just shy of his first birthday, drowned in the family swimming pool. There was nothing instructive about this. Neither Costello nor his wife ever recovered; at the funeral, Mrs. Costello tied and untied the baby's first pair of hard-soled shoes, whispering, "This one I always called my angel."

I had never before known this odd feeling. Something terrible had happened to a man I did not know—a man dead 20 years himself—and I wanted it not to happen. I was full of regret for Abbott and Costello, partly because Jim Mullholland was. You could tell it killed him to have to report on their less funny efforts, to describe their incomprehensible and rarely shown last movie, *Dance with Me Henry*. If only they'd made better movies. If only they could have lived in a world free of dreary love interests. If only Lou Jr. had been rescued. At 11, I imagined that Bud Abbott could have saved him. Wouldn't that have made sense? He loosens his silk tie. He sets his hat on the tiled edge of the swimming pool. Already his slicked-back hair looks wet. Everyone knows that a fully dressed man falling into a pool is funny; the two of them will surface, spouting twin streams of water from their mouths. Then Abbot and Costello would have to stay together forever.

Despite my wishes, they made *Abbott and Costello Go to Mars*. They got in terrible trouble with the IRS. Abbott was an epileptic and an alcoholic; Costello suffered from a bad heart and a bad temper all his life. They aged badly. They argued about money with each other. Lou Jr. fell into the pool and was dead before anyone ever noticed. They split up, and never amounted to anything apart.

That's the inherent sadness to comedy duos: like marriage, they end in death or divorce, they never last forever. Martin and Lewis eventually hated each other, though I have heard Jerry Lewis wept when his old partner died. George Burns missed Gracie Allen for all those years he survived her, a considerable number. The comedy team of Clark and McCullough ended when Bobby Clark picked up his old partner from a sanitarium, took him to a barber shop; there, Paul

McCullough slit his own throat and wrists with a handy razor. Bud Abbott said, upon Lou Costello's death, "My heart is broken. I've lost the best pal anyone ever had," despite the fact they had not spoken to each other in nearly two years.

Even if you ended up hating him, wouldn't you long for that person with whom you were funny and lovable, with whom your name was so aligned, people would have a hard time recognizing your solo unadorned billing?

(Not that comedy teams of three or more aren't also sad in ways. In fact, because so many of them are composed of actual brothers—the Marx Brothers, the Three Stooges [Larry wasn't a relative, but Moe and Curly and Shemp were], the Ritz Brothers—they are sad in another particular, familiar way. I'm not sure I've ever read anything so heartbreaking as Moe Howard writing about the death of his younger brother Jerome, known as Curly).

In the movies, they're together, all of them.

I understand I should have loved Laurel and Hardy instead, or the Marx Brothers. Even the Three Stooges have a campy nostalgic appeal. Abbott and Costello aren't great enough to be art, nor bad enough to be kitsch. No doubt one of the reasons I loved them— still do—is because the book assured me they were underappreciated. Well, I thought, *I'd* appreciate them. It didn't take much effort. There's nothing quite as enticing to a preteen as knowing that disaster is about to happen to a grown man. Here it comes: every time Lou Costello says the words Susquehanna Hat Company to a stranger, he'll be slapped, and the crown of another one of his store of straw hats will be popped from the brim. He knows it, too; he just can't help himself.

I memorized the words to "Who's On First," their most famous routine. I liked to imagine that someday, someone would say to me, casually, the straight man's first line—*The players on our ball team have some funny names: Who's on first, Why's on second, and I-Don't-Know's on third*—and I would answer. I'd be the comic, of course. (George Burns's love for Gracie is legendary; to me, the surest proof is that he'd originally planned to be the comic. When he saw she was funnier, he let her ever be the one who delivered the punchlines.)

I wasn't so generous. I wanted the laughs, and so I dreamt of a straight man. The only thing I knew for sure is that he would say this one thing to me, and we would be able to talk for quite a while, saying things that delighted each other.

In other words, at age 11, I began to wait for love.

Why would anyone dream of meeting her Romeo, his Beatrice, her Alice B. Toklas? Dream of your Hardy, your Abbott, your perfect straight man, your endearing maddening comic, your Gracie Allen who will transform the most casual serious remark into something daffy and lovely.

Look: I'm on a new set, in a fresh new uniform; I'm just starting to wonder what to do with this prop in my hand. You're here, too. I'm a sailor, I'm a ghost, I'm a door-to-door salesman, a cowboy, a soldier; you are my pain-in-the-neck. The only thing I know for sure is that we walk towards that bakery, that house, that policeman on horseback together. It's a bad idea, but we'll do it.

Let me take a look at you. You look fine, friend. Ask me a question.

A LOVE MATCH

MARGOT LIVESEY

MY FIRST AMERICANS came bearing guns, shotguns to be exact, when I was twelve years old. This was in the county of Perthshire, on the edge of the Scottish Highlands. The Americans, with their strange accents and their posh clothes, had flown a huge distance to shoot grouse on Lord Mansefield's moors. Mansefield owned almost as far as the eye could see but, for much of the year, his ownership was irrelevant; we walked across his land as if it were our own. For a few weeks each autumn, however, he became our employer. Rumor had it that the Americans paid a fabulous sum for the privilege of shooting his moors: five hundred pounds a week each. Meanwhile we local children were paid one pound ten shillings a day to work as "beaters." The loaders, sons of local gentry, were paid five pounds a day.

The grouse shooting season opens, by long tradition, on August twelfth, the Glorious Twelfth. That morning we rose at six, made our packed lunches and bicycled to the agreed rendezvous. Soon a decrepit landrover clattered down the road and we squeezed in among dogs, gillies, and other beaters. "Grand weather," someone would remark if it were anything short of the storm scene in *Lear*. We bumped along small roads and farm tracks, climbing into the hills and, eventually, coming to a stop at a steading. Usually we beaters were issued our red flags and set off across the moors immediately. Thick mist or torrential rain might warrant a slight delay but, for obvious reasons, outright cancellation was rare. The guns, who were staying at a fancy hotel ten miles away, would be arriving later after a leisurely breakfast.

Basically we spent the day describing figure eights, the blinds being the apex of the eight. For the first hour we headed out across the moors led by the second gamekeeper or a gillie to some prearranged spot. Then we would fan out at half-mile intervals across the hillside, a line of perhaps five or six miles, with gillies at either end, and begin the walk back.

This was the most peaceful part of the day. My fellow beaters were invisible, the heather was in bloom, and each footstep yielded a subtle fragrance and a cloud of midgies. On fine days the larks hovered overhead singing their intricate song. It was hard in these circumstances to remember that I had a job, but periodically I would wave my red flag and utter a feeble "Hoo, hoo."

Scottish grouse are small-headed, plump-bodied birds, roughly the size of a bantam hen; their tawny plumage is designed for camouflage and their instinct in the face of difficulty is to sit still as long as possible. As I walked along they rose up, almost from beneath my feet, startling me with their barking cries and red-rimmed eyes. Years later, when I saw a statue of a siren in the Villa Gulia in Rome, the plump, feathered body reminded me of a grouse—though their songs, surely, have little in common.

As we drew near the guns, peace vanished. My fellow beaters came into view, waving their flags and shouting. The sky grew crowded with grouse and the shooting started, single shots at first, then erratic volleys. Bodies and pellets fell like rain. In the blinds the

Americans were firing, passing their empty guns to the loaders, and receiving loaded ones in exchange. After a considerable expenditure of ammunition, the slaughter was not as great as one might expect. The Americans for the most part were wretched shots and only the discreet presence of the gamekeepers ensured a respectable bag at the day's end.

Walking into the gunfire, we beaters hoped to be hit. There was a well-established scale of rewards for injury: ten pounds for a limb, fifteen for the torso, twenty-five for the head. A head shot seemed too much of a good thing but a pellet in the arm or leg struck me as good value. I had watched my stepmother digging little bits of blue-black metal out of a rabbit and could easily envision the procedure on myself. It did not occur to me that the rabbit had been dead. Although grouse are low-flying birds and the guns, especially at moments of excitement, often fired without pausing to aim, I never did earn more than thirty shillings a day. Nor, in several seasons, did anyone I knew.

When we reached the blinds there was a welcome pause while the dogs went into action. Beaters were expected to pick up any birds that fell nearby but I always tried to look the other way. Often the grouse were not entirely dead and had to have their necks wrung. Besides, this brief interlude was the closest we got to the Americans and here was a much rarer avis. Some dressed as parodies of the English gentleman in immaculate plus fours and absurdly crisp caps; they did not seem to understand that such clothes are never new. Others wore weirdly light-colored jackets and large, vivid boots. Over and above their clothes, they looked strikingly different from people I knew. For the first time I grasped the distinction between tanned and weather-beaten. In addition several of them wore dark glasses, which I associated exclusively with blindness. (Could this be a clue to their wild marksmanship?) On closer inspection a few of the Americans turned out to be women there for company or to fire their own guns. The loaders grumbled about working for them: more demanding, harder to talk to, and, worst of all, stingy.

While we studied them, the Americans were absorbed in claiming their prey. Occasional altercations broke out: birds could not be found or several people claimed the same corpse. The gamekeepers did their best to make peace. As at a children's party, everyone got a prize. I remember the grouse lined up at the end of the day, brace by brace (a brace is two birds). Typically there would be around sixty with a few hares the keepers hadn't been able to resist thrown in. But, and this was the strangest part of all, in spite of paying so much money, the guns got to keep only a couple of brace each day; the rest belonged to Lord Mansefield and were destined for the night train to London. Tomorrow other rich people would eat them at the Savoy and the Ritz.

As quickly as possible the gillies marshaled us and we set off to walk two or three miles in the opposite direction. Meanwhile the guns drank coffee, chatted, read the paper, and, when we once again appeared on their horizon, simply turned around and shot over our heads. After two drives it was usually lunchtime. The Americans settled down with their picnic hampers. We fantasized about their food; sometimes the pop of corks was audible as we hastily ate our own soggy sandwiches. Then it was time to move on to a different sets of blinds and begin again.

SO MY LONG relationship with America and its inhabitants could scarcely be described as love at first sight. Nor even second, although I must confess to the beginnings of a crush. One rainy night, the Easter I was fourteen, my guardian drove us the ten miles to Perth Odeon. The cinema was cold and smelled of wet raincoats. I had been there once in my entire life, to see *The Sound of Music*. Now I watched in rapt amazement as several tanned Americans, wearing the dark glasses I was learning to think of as ubiquitous, mounted glittering motorcycles and drove across a landscape quite different from our moors and hills. I understood at once that Fonda and Hopper had almost nothing in common with the wealthy hunters of my earlier acquaintance; in their hands the New World seemed a frightening and alluring place. For months afterward I dreamed of *Easy Rider:* the wide skies, the casual intertwining of lives, the violence.

Those images fused with two other early moments in my romance with America. One evening my parents interrupted my homework to make me watch the news of President Kennedy's assassination on our small black and white television. I had read *Julius Caesar* and *Macbeth* but this was the first time I understood that people here, now, in the world, killed kings and leaders. Just as mind-expanding, though in a very different way, were the moon shots, Armstrong bobbing above the lunar desert. In my classrooms the old pink-colored maps from before the Second World War still hung on the walls. Now America was coloring another part of the universe red, white, and blue.

THE TEN MILES to Perth Odeon was a noteworthy journey during my childhood and I did not venture much further afield until I left school. Then, the summer I was eighteen, I went to Paris to work as an au pair for a doctor's family. Although I had studied French since the age of nine, it had not really registered with me that anyone besides Miss Gibson, our French teacher, actually parlez-vous-ed. Now I was surrounded by people chattering nineteen to the dozen in what was clearly not English but which seemed to bear very little relation to the syllables I had dutifully mastered to pass exams. "Bonjour. Je m'appelle Margot. Comment allez-vous? Ça va bien. Merci beaucoup."

The doctor's house was in a courtyard off rue General Duclerc. That first evening, tired from traveling all day, I was thrilled when

Madame explained that I was not actually living *en famille*. Freedom, I thought, as she showed me to a small, green room on the third floor of a building across the courtyard. It was a house of rooms but the only other occupant I knew was the doctor's housekeeper, with whom I shared a toilet and bathroom down the hall. Annie, I now realize, was in her early twenties that summer, scarcely more than a girl herself, but her devotion to duty made her seem much older, not a possible friend.

My duties as an au pair were threefold. I shopped, cleaned, and taught English. Every morning Annie sent me off to the outdoor market with a list and a wad of pretty colored money. I had never seen such lustrous produce, the radiant peaches, the tomatoes like tiny suns; even the butter gleamed with pearly light. Invariably I bought too much—*un kilo* was easier to mime than *un demi kilo*—and could barely carry the basket home.

Annie would chide my excess as she unpacked the groceries, then over a cup of milky coffee detail my chores for the day. It was not so different from home. I hoovered, made beds, dusted, and, several times a week, cleaned the doctor's rather sinister waiting room; only Annie was allowed into the surgery. After lunch I was free until late afternoon when I gave Sylvie, the daughter of the household, her English lesson.

But free to do what? Speechless, alone, my long afternoons weighed heavily. How often can an eighteen-year-old go to the Louvre? And staying in my green room, reading, made me feel like a failure. Growing up in a small rural community, I had not realized that meeting people might be hard. The only problem, I assumed, was a lack of people. If they were there, I would meet them. Now I wandered through the beautiful city, baffled by the crowds. So many, yet no one for me. Then, one happy day, I stumbled upon the American Center on the Boulevard Raspail. My tongue was unlocked; here at last were people I could talk to. I met Americans in droves that summer, not simply holiday-makers but a quite other tribe who had all seen *Easy Rider:* the expatriates. They wore jeans and bandannas, were often accompanied by dogs also wearing the latter, and frequently disparaged Uncle Sam. Many were dodging the draft.

A slight, fair man, with watery hair much longer than mine, befriended me. Rick had spent the last two years living in Berlin and had moved to Paris that spring in search of the remnants of '68. One afternoon he announced he was going to score. You can come along, he said and, only dimly understanding his intentions, I agreed. We took the Metro to the theater where an American production of *Hair* was playing and made our way backstage. In the dressing room, to my amazement, the cast, men and women, black and white, were lounging around naked. They were the most beautiful people I had ever seen. I stared, knowing I shouldn't, but it was clear they didn't care; their nakedness was a kind of altruism, marking them as beings of a higher moral order. Meanwhile Rick discussed quality and quantity. Money passed in one direction; grass in the other. I remember the slightly comic nature of doing business with people with no pockets. As we left for our fifth row seats, they began to put their clothes back on only to take them off a little later, before a thousand people, in the name of art.

The events of that summer, good and bad, largely vanished in the excitement of going to university. I had all but forgotten Rick when in early November an envelope arrived. I stared, baffled, at the enclosed form. Finally I figured out that he had bought life insurance at Charles de Gaulle Airport and named me as his beneficiary. If his plane back to America crashed, I would receive twenty-five thousand dollars. How odd, I thought, how American. In the weeks that followed, without meaning Rick the slightest harm, I occasionally found myself fantasizing about what it would be like to receive such a sum of money—at that time five thousand dollars was enough to buy a little house in the town where I studied—but I never heard from him again.

THE FOLLOWING JUNE I sat on a plane high over the Atlantic reading *On the Road.* Gone were the old books—*Sons and Lovers, Middlemarch, Great Expectations*—all those testimonials to oppressive domesticity and social order. This, I thought, turning the pages of Kerouac, is what it will be like: cars, the open road, and, best of all, freedom from the Victorian attitudes that had dominated my childhood. We landed at Kennedy Airport on an unbelievably hot afternoon. In Scotland when the temperature rose over seventy, we complained that it was boiling. Inside the terminal gruff customs officials, cousins of the guns, posed tricky questions. How did I expect the small amount of money I had with me to last the duration of my visit? Why was I in America? That I was visiting, in a roundabout way, my boyfriend in Toronto only seemed to increase their anxiety. Over and over they counted my travelers' checks and went through my purse. I watched in amazement. In spite of Kerouac my question was, why would anyone want to stay here?

After this difficult start the ugliness of the landscape coming in from the airport was reassuring, not so unlike the shabbiness of North London or that region of France between Calais and Paris. But as we approached Manhattan, or New York as I then called it, everything changed, a new kind of specific density seemed to overtake experience. Could gravity really function amid so many tall buildings? In fact, could any of the natural laws prevail? Here was the antithesis of the moors where you could walk all day and see nothing manmade. In Manhattan it seemed the task might be to find anything *not* manmade.

Through the student organization that had arranged my visa, I had booked a room in a hotel near the Empire State Building. I forget the name but I can still picture the lobby with its palm trees and marble floors. It all seemed intimidatingly grand but as soon as I entered the elevator, the grandeur receded. I found myself occupying a room whose every shabby detail conspired to remind me of my predecessors. I fled downstairs.

It was ten at night and I had been told not to go out in New York alone after dark. Happily the lobby was thronged with people. As I wandered around staring at them, trying to guess which were Americans, a man started talking to me. He was older, from Kansas, and worked, he said, as a naval engineer. I remember his smart brown jacket and his tie. We spoke for a while; he had visited London the year before. Then he asked me something. I didn't understand. He offered money. I didn't understand. He offered more money. We didn't even need to go to my room, he said. Surely there was a quiet place in the lobby.

Later an American friend would translate: the man had offered me three hundred dollars for a blowjob behind the potted palms. Blowjob? Further explanation followed.

In certain crucial ways this first conversation was a blueprint for the many that followed. Wherever I went that summer I used the freedom of a foreigner to talk to people. Only gradually did I begin to grasp that the seemingly common language masked a deep divide. I misunderstood most of what I saw around me, many of the people whom I met. My hosts, genial and otherwise, were no match for my impregnable innocence.

I SPENT MY first couple of days visiting museums and tourist attractions. I was particularly entranced by the snail-like Guggenheim and I dutifully went up in the Empire State Building and took the ferry to Staten Island. What really intrigued me, however, was not one of the masterpieces or the historical monuments but the seemingly un-stoppable mass of people who filled the streets of New York. I had not thought there could be such various colors of skin or clothes. Men and women alike wore rainbow-bright garments—red, yellow, tie-dyed, blue—and everyone under thirty had a McGovern for President button.

The guns seemed to have wholly vanished from this jostling crowd but I soon glimpsed where they might be hiding. After two nights in the hotel, I moved to Scarsdale. I had met Monica in Paris the previous summer where nothing about her pre-Raphaelite hair and bare feet had indicated that she came from a house with pillars and a red carpet rolling from the front door to the pavement. What her parents thought when I appeared at dinner, like Monica, barefoot in my faded jeans, I dread to consider. The only conversation I recall having with her mother was about the exact date of my departure.

Perthshire has more occupied castles per square mile than any county in Britain and I grew up no stranger to stately homes. Usually, however, these places were renowned for their discomfort. They were perpetually damp, freezing all year round, with inadequate plumbing situated far down drafty corridors and furniture which Bonnie Prince Charlie may well have used but not with any ease or pleasure, and their inhabitants were considered victims of misfortune. Over tea in lofty drawing rooms they spoke longingly of bungalows with central heating. So what struck me about Monica's house was not the pillars or the grand piano but the level of comfort. Irrespective of the torrid temperatures outside, the air conditioning made the hair rise on my arms and the sofas and armchairs were so soft I had a hard time not falling asleep when I sat down. I found such luxury delightful but, as a true daughter of reformer John Knox, vaguely reprehensible.

THE MAN I was visiting was away, traveling himself, when I arrived in North America and I had somehow to get through a fortnight before I could see him. My plan, insofar as I had one, was to explore as much of the country as possible. The day after my chat with

Monica's mother found me standing beside a highway, holding out my thumb. Alan, another of my Parisian acquaintances, had invited me to visit him in Athens, Georgia, and, armed with a map, I was going there in the most economical way I knew. I and all my friends hitchhiked in Britain as a matter of both convenience and necessity. Kerouac had led me to believe it was more or less the same here.

By the end of that first day I realized how stupid I had been. Standing beside those enormous roads was both lonely and daunting and the distances between towns was unimaginably large. Not only the geography but the mores of hitching were quite other. Lorry drivers, who in Britain could be counted on for lifts, here seemed oblivious to their obligations. The only truck that did stop was transporting a mobile home. I had never seen such a thing and was sorely tempted to join this little house on its voyage—how amazing this country was—but even to my inexperienced eyes it was the slowest possible means of travel.

And by no means my only alternative. A major source of loneliness was not that people didn't stop but that they did. Late that first day a hearse pulled up beside me with a group of hippies heading for Florida. Athens was on their way, they assured me, absolutely. Their long hair and top hats reminded me of my friends in Paris but something about their glassy-eyed enthusiasm, combined with the mattress in the back of the hearse, made me nervous. Thank you very much, I said, but I'm waiting for someone. They burst out laughing and drove away with a Victory sign. My main rule was never to get into a car with more than one person, which meant, in effect, that I traveled only with solitary men.

As I journeyed south more regional differences became apparent. American drivers, compared to their British counterparts, were staggeringly generous. They would take me to restaurants and buy me meals of immense proportions. I encountered for the first time home fries, grits, pancakes (as opposed to crepes), Jell-O salad, iceberg lettuce, biscuits, the bottomless coffee cup, iced water, iced tea. Afterwards I would dutifully fill out the comment cards. Was the coleslaw excellent, very good, good, fair, or poor? At Morrison's Academy for Girls my report cards had mainly read "fair" so that was how I answered.

Of course people were curious about me. I told them I came from Scotland, was here on my university holidays, traveling around to see as much as I could of the country. I did not mention my more personal reasons for being there. Everyone had their recommendations: you must go to Nantucket; it would be a crime not to visit California; the Grand Canyon—most amazing sight you'll ever see. Often this topic seemed to lead to my finances and several people gave me money. One elderly man, whose maroon car had a bench seat, gave me enough for a hotel room. Several others gave me five or ten dollars.

When they had finished asking me questions my drivers did exactly what I had been told Americans would do. They talked with shocking frankness about health problems, family and romantic difficulties, setbacks at work. Stranger still, it did not seem to matter whether I in turn offered revelations. Their conversation was not measured, a confidence for a confidence, a handful of shame for a handful of guilt. But there was often a price to pay. When it came to the moment to let me off, my drivers sometimes seemed reluctant to part with me. What about dinner? (it was only five in the afternoon, for goodness sake), a visit to their home town? I would feign carsickness, thirst, anything to get them to pull into a rest area where I could seize my rucksack and hurry away.

Like Monica's house, Alan's accommodation turned out to be a surprise. He lived in a mysterious neighborhood where the houses were both too close together and too far apart, my first suburb. The building itself, one story and sprawling, was also unlike anything I knew. We call this a ranch house, Alan explained as he showed me around. I would have called it a poorly planned bungalow. More than location or design, however, it was the situation of Alan and his brother that made the house unusual. They had lost their parents in a car accident a few years before and since then had lived like miniature adults. The summer of my visit Alan was nineteen and about to go to Stanford; his brother was twenty-three. What made their quasi-adult life possible was the presence of their housekeeper, a plump, smiling woman named Mary. I had grown up with cooks and cleaners at the boys' school where my father taught but there was one firm rule: never let them wait on you. More to the point perhaps none of them would have offered to do so. Now when I appeared in the morning, Mary offered coffee. How would you like your eggs, honey? she asked.

The whole situation made me uneasy. For most of my eighteen years I had been desperately seeking to escape the thrall of adults. I gave up eating breakfast and, one evening at a bar, asked Alan whether he didn't share my feelings. Why didn't he get his own meals, wash his own clothes? Didn't he want to be independent? He was impatient and mystified. I've known Mary all my life, he said. We pay her. Quickly I produced some of my hitchhiking money and offered to buy more drinks.

By the end of my visit to Athens I couldn't face more open roads. Using some of my precious travelers' checks, I flew back to New York and boarded a Greyhound bus to Chicago. I spent most of the journey sitting beside a pleasant young man who did downers. He was on his way to Cleveland to visit an uncle. Joe's helping me get back on track, he said, his vague gesture somehow suggesting that this was a large undertaking. When we reached the city, he invited me to stop off for a couple of days but, in spite of Kerouac, Scottish thrift prevailed. I had a ticket to Chicago and to Chicago I would go. Years later when I finally did visit Cleveland as a writer-in-residence I wondered what it would have been like if I had taken him at his word. I think that was the year the Cuyahoga caught fire.

We arrived in downtown Chicago at six o'clock on a very hot evening. I found a pay phone, something that could take half an hour in London but here was accomplished in a matter of minutes, and rang the only people I knew in the entire metropolis. I'm a friend of your friend Nancy, I explained. I had no contingency plan but none was needed. Forty minutes later Ben and Rebecca showed up at the bus station, having driven down from Evanston to collect me. Rebecca had long straight hair and wore a tie-dye t-shirt, jeans, and sandals. Ben had dark curly hair and was similarly dressed. They both had brown eyes, which I considered exotic, and so did the two small children in the back of their elderly car. They insisted I sit in front to see the view.

Rebecca and Ben lived in a second-floor apartment on a pleasant tree-lined street in Evanston, only a few blocks from Northwestern University where he taught and she studied. I remember Rebecca that first evening showing me around the kitchen with the intensity of a museum guide. It was the first American home into which I'd been truly welcomed and I marveled at the size of everything: the fridge tall as a person; the jar of peanut butter large enough to stop a charging rhino. "What's ours is yours," she said, smiling at me.

Ben and Rebecca were open not only in their hospitality but, as I soon came to appreciate, in their marriage. Rebecca's boyfriend came over most evenings and would babysit for the children while the three of us went out to supper. Never in Scotland, I thought. They seemed to have almost no connection with their gun-bearing compatriots. Presently I realized, only because they told me, that they were Jewish. Oh, I said, how wonderful. For years I had read about Jewish people in my Scottish Sunday school but I had never, knowingly, met any before.

Of course this turned out to be yet another occasion on which I misunderstood almost everything. One night I woke to find Rebecca's boyfriend sitting on the edge of my bed, taking off his shoes. What are you doing? I asked. You know, he said. I can't remember how I managed to persuade him to put his clothes back on and leave the room but in the morning it was clear that some credo had been broken. Rebecca no longer smiled as she poured my orange juice. Ben did not invite me to accompany him to the library. It was not like hitchhiking where my drivers told me the secrets of their hearts and I talked about the British royal family. I had accepted hospitality and, when called upon, had failed to return it; I had clung to the superiority of an observer rather than risking the moral ambiguity of a participant. I left the next day, catching an airplane and flying to Toronto to see the man I had come to see all along.

THOSE FEW CROWDED weeks certainly made an impression on me but no deeper, I would have claimed, than the winter I spent in Tunisia or the summer in Edinburgh. Oh, yes, America, I would say fondly when it came up in conversation. I've been there. Sometimes I would tell a brief anecdote or voice an opinion but I was always anxious to make clear that I did not share the global fascination with this country. I had had my fling with America but my heart was quite intact. Seven years later I was surprised to discover how pleased I was when the man I was living with took a job in Los Angeles.

We drove across the country from Toronto and rented a shabby house in Venice, in those days a neighborhood still perilously balanced between funk and hip, bohemian and chic. By this time tie-dye had given way to punk and I surveyed the crowds on the boardwalk with fascination. When I couldn't bear the sight of one more roller skater with a mohawk, I went and stood by that endless body of water known as the Pacific and gazed out toward Japan.

Maybe if I were lucky the grunion would run tonight as they do so memorably in *The Last Tycoon.*

In Paris during the summer of the expatriates, I had read Sartre's account of love: the Self and the Other connected by the gaze. America, from those first gunshots on the moors, was vastly Other and in that otherness I gradually began to find myself. By the time I came to Venice, I had spent years trying to write fiction without ever quite managing to implement Auden's shatteringly simple advice: write about what interests you. Now, sitting in a little house on Superba Avenue, I stared past the palm tree I had planted in the front garden and wrote a story called "Obituary" set five thousand miles away in the town of Pitlochry where I had spent several excruciatingly boring summers of my childhood. By this time my parents were both dead and the story said something that mattered to me profoundly. Best of all, it was taken from what I had previously seen as the humdrum material of my life. I had gazed at the Other and found the Self.

FOR YEARS WHEN my British friends described me as living in America, I balked. I don't live there, I'd tell them. I just spend a lot of time there. But usually they weren't listening; they were already launched into their litany of complaints. It's such a narcissistic country and so violent. You know they still have the death penalty. I've never seen so many beggars as in New York and they're almost all black. (Even though London too now has a large number of people on the streets, the homeless tend to share the complexion of the majority of the population.) I nodded and agreed with their accusations. I even added my own. But recently, I can't say exactly when or why, something odd has occurred. I no longer deny that I live here. My relationship with America, which I've long claimed as a matter of convenience, has turned into something else. What began as a fling and became a marriage of convenience has grown into a love match.

A PLEA FOR CHAOS

DENNIS McFARLAND

A RECENT SUNDAY, a farewell brunch with our buddies on the block, John and Laurie: in a couple of weeks, we'll be moving out of our suburban house and into an apartment building in the next town over—where the kids can walk to school, where somebody's paid to shovel the snow, where life (we hope) will be simpler. Today Laurie has urged us to leave the kids at home for a couple of hours, now that the kids are just barely old enough for that, and get out for a little "adult conversation"—not the clever chatter with a racy ping the term implies, but any talk on any subject in which you're allowed to finish a sentence without being interrupted by an eight-year-old. Michelle, my wife, has chosen the restaurant, a converted bank building, for its close proximity to home; if there were an emergency, we could be home in ten minutes. On this cold blue-sky day in February, sunlight pours through the restaurant's tall windows. The food is okay, and there's plenty of it. We've been yakking about one thing and another when, about midway through the meal, there's a quiet commotion at the table behind me—a sort of crucial expiration of breath followed by a scuffling of chairs. John and I are facing our wives who now gaze past us to whatever's happening at our backs; Laurie's eyes impart a warning—"Don't turn around"—and when at last I say, "What is it?" she whispers, "There's someone very sick at the table right behind you." Immediately I experience a visceral repulsion having to do with *sick* and *restaurant omelets*, but then I catch sight of Michelle's eyes, which have watered over with the explicit look that signifies her heart's going out.

Over the next five minutes, we witness a frail, emaciated young man (no older than thirty) being helped to the back of the dining room, into a wide hallway, and situated on the floor with folded tablecloths for padding beneath him. I easily identify the members of the party—frail young man, frail young man's partner, frail young man's parents—and determine with equal ease that the young man is in the advanced stages of AIDS. His mother and father are perhaps in their late fifties, and there's something touching about the way they've put on nice clothes for this Sunday brunch with their son and his partner. Of course the atmosphere in the restaurant has changed profoundly, but the staff and the other diners try to carry on as if tragedy weren't blooming just a few feet from their festive mimosas. I can't seem to hear what John and Laurie are saying. I've become obsessed with two tiny orange medicine tablets that lie abandoned next to a glass of water at the place where the young man sat, and every few seconds I meet Michelle's eyes, a risky business, since we're both fighting back tears. If my wife and I were alone, I'm not sure what we would say to each other. Something has happened we didn't expect. With little more than a sigh, a window has slipped open, it is night, a biting wind blows, sorrow, loss.

Soon EMTs arrive and take charge, and soon the young man, followed by his partner and his mother, is carried out of the restaurant on a stretcher. Soon the father is back at the table, hurriedly gathering coats and scarves. I turn to him and point out the medicine tablets on the table. (Maybe a pill will save him!) The father thanks me quickly, then pauses to look me in the eye. He appears confused—he has the florid complexion of someone too long exposed to the elements—and his looking at me seems partly accidental and partly a kind of impulsive experiment; he's surprised to find himself peering into the face of another man, someone he doesn't know. In that instant, I imagine that I recognize him. I stammer, "I hope . . . I hope . . ." and seeing the blind alley I've turned down, the father shakes his head. When he speaks, he speaks very softly and leans toward me. Still shaking his head, he says, "He's just so sick." It's a father's midnight remark, probably to his wife, about the baby, and here, in this moment, he has uttered it with a tone that says not that he finds this station at which his family has arrived—after the intricate journey of more than thirty years—incredible, nor even unbearable. The man is saying he finds it impossible.

THE WORK OF the EMTs required the restaurant doors to be open for a bit, and afterward, frigid air lingered in the dining room—the last physical detail I can recall about the brunch. I can not say what happened next, or next, or next. What I know is that Michelle and I were surely eager to get home to the kids, and that for most of the day I was pensive, plodding around in a spiritual marsh, often sad, just as often grateful. The father's face—its registering of impossible, irrevocable outcomes—stayed with me, has stayed with me still; that day, it seemed to lodge like a sharp pin in my rib cage, threatening to nick a lung should I try taking a really full breath. And somewhere in the course of things I beheld the great gift of companionship, my family, our friends, their inestimable seeing-through value.

I thought of my wife's closest and oldest friend, Garnet, who was killed at the age of thirty-nine by a rapid, savaging cancer. I thought of a book she gave me: Mirabel Osler's *A Gentle Plea for Chaos*, which urges, among other proposals, putting back the country in England's country gardens. Garnet, a poet, not a gardener, probably didn't care a lot about the state of England's country gardens (though if she'd been in England, standing near one, she would likely have cared more than most). She gave me the book, seven years ago, because it was my birthday, and because she'd begun the blitz of profitless therapies that would subjugate the rest of her life, and because practically everything in the book seemed metaphorical. Passages about trying not to exert too much control over the natural course of things, about finding beauty where everything has apparently run wild, passages about the indispensable gifts of fellow gardeners all read as if they were written in code, artfully conveying their hidden meanings to the initiated.

I thought of John and Laurie, that other family everyone should have, right on the block, to whom you can turn when, for example, your wife is about to give birth at two A.M., in November, and you need somewhere for your five-year-old daughter to sleep the rest of the night. (As I back the car into the street, Katharine, only half-awake, cries, in real anguish, "Kitty got out! Kitty got out!" and in the sixty seconds it takes me to drive to John and Laurie's, Michelle, cruising down from a particularly sharp contraction, lies, convinces her that what she saw was a leaf blown by the wind and not a cat.) Never mind that John, a lawyer, is fired by such plain hatred for injustice that when he tells you about his current case, his voice rises to a shout and he begins poking you on the arm to emphasize a point; never mind that soon, though you're agreeing with every word, he's giving you flat-palmed jabs to the shoulder that threaten to knock you to the ground. When we brought our new baby home from the hospital, Thanksgiving Day, John had shoveled the snow from our drive and sidewalks. Laurie had left a Thanksgiving picnic for us. Jim and Betsy, a couple in their sixties living next door, arrived with flowers and myriad offers of help. Michelle's mother flew in from Texas and brought with her Michelle's great-uncle, Sam, for whom we'd named the baby. (As he comes through the front door, he says, "Well, you certainly know how to get a person's attention.") I wish the connection between Michelle and her mother were less fraught with old fears and resentments, that the visit didn't need to be so brief; but still, her mother came, and she bore Uncle Sam's travel expenses.

And I thought of the troublesome months before the baby was born. During the first trimester of Michelle's pregnancy, we took up with a young obstetrician through our health plan who had the way-indoors pallor and grim disposition of someone who slept in a casket. See him grinning as he says to his assistant, "Mrs. McFarland is going to generate some urine for you now." Michelle was thirty-seven, and we'd decided to forego the prebirth testing that would reveal the baby's gender and assure us of the baby's normal development. Michelle was precise and certain about when she had become pregnant, but when the doctor first massaged her stomach, he questioned her accuracy and insisted on her getting an ultrasound to "help us sort out the birthdate." Michelle seemed to think that even if she was wrong, which she wasn't, the baby would get born on the day the baby got born. But the doctor, amused by this naive logic, assured her that the test was simple and even fun; he encouraged us to bring along our daughter because older siblings-to-be often found it helpful seeing a picture of what was to come.

On the set day, we manage to find the building, attached to the hospital, where ultrasounds are conducted. A young woman, who identifies herself as a student technician, shows us to a room about the size of a walk-in closet where there is an examination table and the ultrasound equipment; the videoscreen, on which the technician will view the imaging, is cleverly positioned above and behind Michelle's head, so—once Michelle is undressed, flat on her back on the table, and her swollen belly jellied up—she has to twist her neck and strain to see any of the action. Katharine and I are wedged together between the table and the wall, Michelle is visibly cold, the whole experience shrieks of insensibility and waste, and then suddenly the black-and-white flotsam on the screen coheres into the unmistakable, extraterrestrial image of the baby, kicking to beat the band inside Michelle's womb. Every complaint dissolves, doused by this marvel into its proper perspective. There's laughter, followed by a hush and the happy observation of reverence in our daughter's eyes. It seems our purpose has been fulfilled with relative ease, with a little unexpected awe thrown in for good measure. Michelle is first to notice that this feeling of mission-accomplished isn't apparently shared by the young technician, who continues to worry the Ouija-like transducer over Michelle's stomach. At last, Michelle says, "Is everything all right? Everything's all right, isn't it?"

The tech beams a reassuring smile and says, "I'm not really allowed to say anything to you. The doctor will be in soon."

"But everything's all right, isn't it?" Michelle repeats.

The tech evades the question again with a remark about the doctor's superb credentials. She refers to the doctor as the "Cadillac of Ultrasound," an unsettling sobriquet, more machine than human, a world-view lurking inside it that smacks of flash and status, and I'm suddenly fearful. When I lean forward enough to see Michelle's face in the dim glow, I see I'm lagging way behind her in this regard. "Find out what's wrong," she whispers.

With more firmness than I actually intend, I say to the young woman, "What's going on?"

"Nothing to worry about," she says, smiling that smile again. "I'm just not seeing everything I want to see yet. I'm still fairly new to this, you know."

But then she rises from her stool and abruptly leaves the room.

In this brief intermission, I say something to Michelle about this giving new meaning to the expression, "practicing medicine..." about the outrageousness of "the system..." I know people have to learn, but do they have to make everyone feel like guinea pigs? If she's not back in five minutes...

The young technician returns, bringing someone with her, another woman, older, not the doctor, but a supervisor of some sort, who, without the formality of an introduction, begins the procedure all over again while the student stands observing. No one says a word. The new woman circuits the transducer over and over Michelle's belly, pressing deeper and deeper, as if she's trying to erase some indelible riddle.

"Hmm," she says at last, apparently in conclusion.

With unthinkable composure, Michelle quietly asks, "Is there anything wrong?"

"Everything's fine," says the woman, "I just think the doctor should take a look," and then they both leave the room.

Katharine asks me if the baby is going to have hair and teeth when he's born, quickly adding, "Or when *she's* born."

The door opens again, and this time the Cadillac herself leads a pack that includes the two other women and three new people. Now, what had been only a nascent dreamlike air becomes full-blown. No doubt the strange lighting contributes, but as the doctor runs the transducer over Michelle's stomach—with appreciably more authority than we've seen before—the sycophantic hovering at the doctor's shoulders makes me think of angels, of supernatural messengers, and some secret, never-committed part of me takes flight. I can see that Michelle is already crying, and I wonder, as if in a dream, whether or not I should take Katharine out of the room, but then surely if that were called for someone would have suggested it or perhaps even offered to . . .

"There *is* a problem with the baby," the doctor is saying, and I notice for the first time, though I don't entirely trust myself on this, that the doctor's dark hair is cut into the exact shape of Katharine's biking helmet in the coat closet at home. The doctor has frozen an image on the screen and stepped over to it in order to cite details with the pushbutton end of a ballpoint pen. In a breathtakingly neu-

tral tone she explains that the baby's left arm ends just below the
elbow, that this defect is unalterable, and that Michelle, at three
months, is still "well within the framework for an abortion."

Then I become aware of several things at once, and their collective force pulls me back into the room, into the present moment,
into my proper place: somehow one of Michelle's hands has ended
up clutching one of mine; my daughter has begun to cry (politely,
unobtrusively, pressing the side of her head against my right hip),
and the sadness and distress on Michelle's face has been supplanted
by what looks like terror.

"Is there something else?" she's saying, her voice faltering. "Something besides the arm?"

"No, no," says the doctor. "Just the limb anomaly."

"But you said 'abortion.'" says Michelle.

The doctor shrugs her shoulders. "I only wanted you to have all
the information," she says. "To know your options."

And then, most dreamlike of all, the doctor turns and heads for
the door, the coterie first clearing a path, then following her out; a
young man, last to leave, steals a forbidden glance at us before closing
the door.

Michelle and I seek immediate refuge in comforting Katharine,
but soon it appears that, though Michelle is still lying cold on the
table with lubricant smeared on her stomach, nobody's going to come
back into the room. At last I say, "I'll go find out what we're supposed to do."

The glaring bright hallway is empty. I turn one direction and
then the other. Turning a third time, I see the Cadillac of Ultrasound
standing alone at the extreme end of the hallway, reading something
on a clipboard. I'm oddly hopeful as I approach her, feeling lucky to
have so quickly found the highest official. When I reach her, she's
surprised to see me.

"What do we do now?" I ask her.

She underinterprets the question: "Oh, you can go home," she says and returns her eyes to the clipboard. Back inside the small room, I tell Michelle and Katharine that the doctor says we can go home.

THROUGHOUT THAT SPRING I wake in the middle of the night and lie stock-still, silent for what feels like hours; eventually I realize that Michelle, beside me in bed, is awake, too, also lying silent, and we hold each other and cry. During daylight hours, the missing tooth in a comb commands my attention, the broken-off wooden gate-rail at the toll plaza on the Mass. Pike. As I watch the Red Sox on TV, the camera pans the crowd in the stands—sixty thousand fans? eighty thousand?—all of whom have two arms each.

Katharine, finding us silent at the kitchen table, says, "It's not like the baby's dead or something . . ." and Michelle and I say, each in our turn, "That's right," "That's right."

Susan, on the phone from Brooklyn, says, "Believe me, the baby's going to have all the really important things he needs. Wonderful parents, Katharine, a great home . . . I mean, look at *us*. We had all our arms and legs and look how *we* turned out . . . look at the therapy bills."

My mother assures me that she will include us and the baby in the prayers of her prayer circle at the church, and then hastily gets off the line, thinking that if she cries, it won't be helpful and she'll feel ashamed; my father doesn't manage to come to the phone, but weeks later, when I phone home and he answers, he says, "I've tried to call you . . ." I relate his remark to Michelle with some small amount of bitterness, pointing to our answering machine, and she says, "But don't you see . . . that's just what he means . . . he's *tried* to call you."

Alice, from the West Coast, writes a letter—the letter itself significant since for a less important matter she would phone—which begins, "Dear dear Michelle and Dennis, This is what I think (a quite clear vision)—you will have an absolutely extraordinary, amazing child. Person."

Annie, who is unmarried and who also happens to be pregnant— her first, the father, briefly encountered, adamantly forswearing both Annie and the baby—sends a card; she describes a scene she saw in her head: "...my kid scrutinizing your kid, saying 'Where's your arm?' Your kid shrugging, saying, 'I don't know. Where's your dad?'"

And Garnet, with some trepidation, confesses to mixed emotions; the great, spellbound romance of her life was with a boy in college, quarterback of the football team, whose left arm ended just below the elbow; this boy used to tell people his favorite novel was *A Farewell to Arms*; he used to tell people he had a twin brother with three arms. "I've tried," Garnet says, reaching across a table for Michelle's hand, "but I can't quite get sad."

In June, a subsequent amniocentesis tells us the baby's DNA is normal, and that the baby is a boy.

I IMAGINE AN ingenious bridge, made of rope and wooden treads of varying widths, spanning the deep gulch of summer: For July and August we rent a house on a lake in Vermont, a small house, but situated on a bluff overlooking the water, and with a lovely screened porch equipped with a glider and plenty of rocking chairs. A narrow rocky path descends the hill to the water's edge, a hill overgrown with a tangle of briery vines, and when we first arrive, any time we undertake the path, there's the gruesome sibilance of snakes fleeing our feet. After a few days, the snakes flee us entirely, unwilling to put up with the regular nervewracking intrusion of these new white beasts on their hill. Though the lake's actual name is Greenwood, we christen it "Lake Weedybottom," for like all the lakes in Vermont, its floor is a swaying slime of plant life. There's a flow of friends to the little house—Ira comes for a few days from Boston; as do Fred and Linda; and Bev and her boy Katharine's age; Rodger and Moira and their kids all the way from Baton Rouge; and the Vermonters, Francis and Ellen, and Joyce. There are cookouts and card games and canoeing, baths for the kids in the kitchen sink, an orange vagabond cat who brings disemboweled mice to our doorstep, magnificent thunderstorms and a lunar eclipse. The kindness of friends seems kinder somehow, more precious, here, now. Their annoying traits, their minor shortcomings, their occasional thoughtlessness feels intolerable, unbearable, unforgivable.

At night, in bed, my ear pressed against Michelle's stomach, I begin to see that the sadness I feel about the baby's arm is not explicitly about the baby's arm, not explicitly about its presence or absence. My sadness is about a father's wanting his child to have everything the child needs, about a father's wanting to be able to provide, and here I confront the impossibility of that: I will never ever be able to give this child his left arm, no matter how much money I make, no matter how successful I become, no matter how hard I work. I can not even cut off my own arm and give him that, which I would do without hesitation. In the simplest terms, I begin to see that my sadness is, of course, about me and not about the baby.

In August, Garnet, godmother to Katharine, godmother-to-be to Sam, phones from New York. Unable entirely to cloak her panic, she tells us her doctor has discovered a sizable lump in her right breast. About a year and a half from now, a year and a half of sheer hell on earth—of hospitals, radical mastectomy, radiation, autologul bone-marrow transplantation, and chemotherapy; of quarantines and failing protocols; of oozing sores and IV-site infections and shingles; of humiliating financial struggles, housing struggles, employment struggles; of crazy, inexplicable purchases in Manhattan wig stores; of agonizing pain and vomiting and angry collisions with jaded insurance-company clerks and fickle, opportunist oncologists—she will die. Most appalling, she will die far away from us, and on the eve of her wedding.

IT IS JANUARY 17, 1991, a Thursday. The baby we brought home Thanksgiving Day is now fourteen months old, and I've just gotten him and Katharine down for the night; I sit in our bedroom at home, watching on the television the astonishing arcs of white light against a night sky that are the first Patriot theatre antiballistic missiles fired by allied troops into Iraqi territory, the beginning of Operation Desert Storm. Michelle has been in New York the past three days, helping Garnet's fiancé, Earl, pack up Garnet's apartment. Michelle took a room at a hotel nearby and has phoned me nightly to see how we're doing without her and to unload some of the sorrow of the day's events in New York. After an on-again, off-again romance of many years, Garnet and Earl have decided to be married, Garnet wants to move back to the small southern town where she grew up, have her wedding there, and now, though she can't walk from her bed to the bathroom without sitting down to rest, she and Earl are planning to fly down to Arkansas the next day. (We all fear that the trip will kill her, and Earl and Michelle talked Garnet into consulting her doctor about it—feeling certain that he would tell her not to go— but the doctor disappointed us.) Tonight, Michelle is flying back home to Boston, but as I watch the troubling images on the TV, she phones to say that her plane was unable to land in Boston due to fog; they were unable to return to New York because so many other flights were having to return to New York, and so, for now, they have landed in Albany. The passengers have been told that they will probably return to New York, but no one seems to know exactly when, and there's also a chance the fog will lift enough for them to go on to Boston. Michelle wants me to phone the hotel where she stayed and see if she can get back into a room there.

"Have you heard what's happening?" I ask her.

"Oh, yes," she says, "the pilot announced it on our flight," and then she bursts into tears. "I'm not crying about the goddamned war," she says quickly.

"I know," I say.

"It's all so fucking horrible."

"I know."

"I'll call you back when I know something. When *somebody* knows something. *If* anybody ever does."

About an hour later, the phone rings again—Garnet this time, wondering if I've heard anything from Michelle. I begin to explain about the fog and Albany, but she interrupts and says, "I know about that. She called us too. I was wondering if you've heard anything else, since then."

"No," I say. "I just hope she gets home tonight."

There's a brief silence, after which Garnet says, "I know it's selfish of me, but *I* hope she comes back to New York."

Of course it's not selfish to want your closest friend beside you for a few more hours when you're terminally ill, but her expression of this reasonable desire does seem selfish in Garnet, only because it's so uncharacteristic.

"Well, whatever happens," I say, "we'll see you on Sunday."

"That's right," she says and giggles. "My wedding."

"How's Earl?"

"Earl, how are you?" she says off the line. Then, "He's fine. He says to say *our* wedding."

"How do you feel?"

"I've felt better."

"I bet you have."

"But not any time very recently," she adds. "How is beautiful Katharine?"

"Okay. Tired of me, I think."

"Hard to imagine," she says. "And equally beautiful Sam?"

I suddenly think of Katharine's fifth birthday party—eight screaming meemies from her kindergarten class, two months ago—which Garnet attended, and how, in all the photographs of the occasion, Garnet seems to be holding Sam; that was the role she took on for the duration of the party. By then, she'd given up on wigs—gone what she called "wig-crazy," a disorder climaxing in the enigmatic purchase of a very expensive African American wig (Garnet was white). She'd taken to wearing turbans instead, turbans and silk scarves, effecting an ironically spirited result. After the party, after Garnet had left to go back to New York, after the kids were in bed, Michelle went upstairs for a bath. A few minutes later, I found her there, sitting in the tub, sobbing. She looked at me and said what no one had yet said aloud: "She's dying."

"Sam's okay, too," I say to Garnet now, on the telephone.

"Call me if you hear anything," she says.

"I will," I say. "Was your visit all right?"

"With Michelle?" she says. "It was wonderful . . . *she's* wonderful. But of course you know that. You and I couldn't possibly be friends if you didn't."

After this conversation I find myself hoping Michelle's plane returns to New York, but about three hours later it lands in Boston.

The next day, Friday, Garnet arrives at the airport in Arkansas so dehydrated that she's driven in an ambulance directly to the emergency room of the local hospital. There she's "stabilized," and it's everyone's hope that the wedding will go off as scheduled on Sunday afternoon. Michelle and I have made arrangements with a babysitter to stay with the kids so we can fly down Sunday morning, go to the wedding, spend the night, and come back on Monday. Saturday morning, I call any number of florists in Arkansas until I find one that can get two dozen white roses over to Garnet's brother's house, where she and Earl will be staying when Garnet's out of the hospital.

I ask the florist to write, in the note card, "Wishing you much joy on your wedding day."

Knowing we're to leave first thing Sunday morning, and wanting to help out, Jim and Betsy have us and the kids next door for dinner Saturday night. Afterward, when we return home, there's a message on the answering machine from Earl: "Hi . . . it's Earl . . . just call me."

The next morning, Sunday, the taxi driver who arrives to take us to the airport has a bright red-lettered sticker on the bumper of his cab that reads, "Kick Saddam's Butt." We didn't have to make any changes in any of our travel arrangements; it's just that now we will attend a funeral instead of a wedding.

The small-town doctor in Arkansas had tried to relocate Garnet's intravenous site in her thigh, and soon after the procedure, she went into death throes. This took her by surprise, and, fed up with hospitals and hospital workers, she'd done some desperate yelling near the end: "Get out . . . get out . . . can't you see I'm dying!" There was more unpleasantness than even this, but Earl couldn't seem to speak about it.

Apparently, Earl did have time to rush to the brother's house, get the wedding ring, return to the hospital room, and, after more than a decade of ambivalence in this area, exchange hurried marriage vows with Garnet just before she died. I can barely fathom this—it's like an image in a dream that dissolves, repeatedly, the moment before it coheres.

Afterward, when he returned again to the house, Earl found our two dozen roses on the stoop. I believe he had the good sense not to open the card.

THE VAPOR OF loss the small town exuded might actually have had its roots in the Civil War. An active railroad, unconnected to any of the town's own industry, ran right across a littered and decrepit Main

Street; the stench of a paper mill pervaded the air; the schools looked like prisons. The guest house we booked into looked like a whorehouse decorated by Laura Ashley. Its owner, operator, and host turned out also to be the town's mayor, a defeated-looking man in his fifties whose wife had recently divorced him on grounds of mental cruelty. And outside in the cold cold street, as I retrieved the last of our bags from a rented Ford Tempo, I bumped into the town's dogcatcher, a wizened ex-hippie who chain-smoked and poured out his heart: actually, he had always liked dogs; his young children despised him for the work he did; he suffered recurring, calamitous dreams in which he heard the howling of wolves.

In these descriptions there's the remnant of a tone that was, during our brief visit, my mainstay; I climbed up onto a high spiritual bluff, from which I could criticize everything in sight—the garish funeral home, the ineloquent preacher, the dreary food and drunkenness at the wake—and I was generally unhelpful to my grieving wife. Garnet would have deplored the way I behaved in her hometown, though, of course, if she'd been there, alive, I would never have behaved that way. Her great gift, and her gift to others, was that she could so guilelessly admire what was best in a person, and so encourage it.

Michelle concealed any disappointment I may have caused her in Arkansas, perhaps she excused it—under the circumstances, she wasn't about to be detoured by my petty flaws of character: she concentrated throughout on Garnet and the irreplaceable nature of their long friendship. Then, when it was all over and we began the long flight home, she went sound asleep—astonishing me, since the plane was full of rowdy college students returning to school after winter break. Long afterward, when recalling these events, I commented on her surprising ability to sleep during the flight. She told me that when she got on the airplane, all she wanted was the comfort of oblivion, and that, though she wasn't entirely sure about this, oblivion felt, somehow, earned. She told me she'd asked Earl for a sleeping pill and had taken it right after we boarded the plane.

ABOUT THREE AND a half years later, an autumn afternoon: there's a nostalgic chill in the air, quickly recognizable, but not quite as poignant as in former years: I sit at the long wooden picnic table in our backyard, taking a sort of inventory of the signs of change I can observe from this one spot—the tomato plants against the foundation wall of the porch, grown gargantuan, way out of their cages, tied up now to some old steel fence posts I found in the garage; the great horse-chestnut tree, beginning now to drop its brown-spotted leaves and spiny-husks, its barren shady side offering a view of the inner limbs, vaulting like the beams and rafters of a cathedral; the lower path of the sun, the acute angle of its light; and, beyond the weathered stockade fence, the neighbor, Jim, over seventy now and dressed in his crossing-guard's uniform, carefully easing into his car...

I bought this picnic table at a discount department store and had to borrow Jim's station wagon and tie it upside-down to the luggage rack in order to get it home; the benches were set a bit too far away from the table, so I moved them closer, sawed off the resulting stubs of two-by-four, and painted the whole thing dark green. I positioned it on a level patch mid-yard. I was fond of saying to friends, "Doesn't it look just like summer camp?" and more often than not I got back a kind, tolerant smile. I don't know, honestly, if I ever encountered a table like this at summer camp, and in any case, my real memories of summer camp are not especially pleasant ones, though I count among them my first French kiss, which coincided, curiously enough, with my first true romance. But somehow I've connected the look of this table with my youth, and I've taken pains to reconstruct it in my backyard, as if any connection with my youth, regardless of how small or inauthentic, were inherently valuable. And this, I see at last, is the most arresting sign of change: my youth is just that lost.

A few weeks ago, I stopped drinking—the advice of a doctor—and now I need to go to England, to research a book I want to write; I've worried about how I'll fare, alone, anonymous, on the same island where single-malt Scotch whiskey was invented. Not well, I've concluded, and so, an hour earlier, I asked my friend, Tellis, to make the trip with me. I popped the question to him here, at this table, and I made a very big deal of it. The asking made me feel needy and weak, unmanly, as if I were asking him to come along and hold my hand. At the same time, I felt grateful to have Tellis to ask. All the lengthy explaining I did was entirely unnecessary. He knows me, he understands the situation, yet he listened patiently as I managed to blow on and on and never actually put the proposition in the form of a question. In some ways, our sitting here at the same table is unlikely—it's unlikely (though we are the same age) that we should be friends at all, given our very different backgrounds: I grew up in the South, he in the North; I went to college and avoided military service, he went to Vietnam right out of high school; I'm white, he's black. And yet, here we were, as close as any brothers could be. I imagine this has something to do with his entering my life through my children, with his starting out as babysitter to the kids. Very soon, we had the common ground of their behavior and care and welfare—a scrappy terrain that proved teeming with reflecting pools: we would begin by talking about something one of the kids had done and how we'd responded; we would end up talking about the often distressing things we'd seen about ourselves in it and drawing comparisons to what *our* fathers would have done. Today, at the picnic table, when I finally finished with all my exposition and apology and wayward detail, Tellis shrugged his shoulders and said, "Let's roll."

And now, having seen the clear specter of my lost youth, I don't want to rush to the nearest Chevrolet dealer and price the red Stingray in the showroom; I want to see my kids. I look at my wristwatch to see how long it will be before they're home from school. I want to believe that whatever I can give to my children, what they carry from me into the future, if it has a quality to sustain them, then that gives value to the past. I want to believe nothing valuable is ever really lost—not entirely, anyway—it's merely clarified down to its essence, making it portable, and then passed on. All these journeys life requires of us, those we volunteer for, those we're persuaded into, those we're forced on against our wills—what can be said of them? Could it be this: that we traveled together, profiting from one another's company, that there was some intimacy along the way?

LAST WEEK, I took my daughter, now going on thirteen, to Mt. Auburn Cemetery to find the gravestone of a classmate who had drowned two years earlier. We found the boy's stone—the wonderful boy's stone—and she stood before it, unblinking, defiant, as if she would annihilate the granite with the sheer intensity of her refusal to look away, her refusal to be *moved*. What she felt strongest when Garnet died was betrayal, life's, of her sense that the people we rely on will return to us. Garnet's death made her angry, and in that particular regard she's angry still. It's a distinct anger, well-defined, and I spotted it again as she stood before her classmate's stone in the cemetery. But then we noticed a man nearby, alone, standing in the middle of the bordering lane, lost for a moment and casting about with his eyes, then walking over to sit on a nearby bench. When we saw his shoulders begin to shake, Katharine reached for me; she wanted an arm about her, a natural inclination.

On my recent pensive Sunday, after Michelle and I returned home from brunch with John and Laurie, Tellis dropped by with a fishing pole he'd made for Sam: a good rod and reel, customized with a short length of PVC, attached with duct tape; the extension of the rod, below the reel, made it easy for Sam to grip the thing between his side and his short arm, leaving his hand free for reeling. Tellis was having trouble again with his girlfriend. "She's been really depressed," he told me when we were alone in the kitchen. "So I went out and bought her a really expensive lens for her camera. And did it make one bit of difference? No."

"Tellis," I say, as gently as I can. "That would probably have worked if she was depressed about not having enough lenses for her camera."

He looks stumped for a moment, then says, "Oh yeah. Good point."

Later, Betsy drops by to see if we can watch their dog overnight; one of the grandkids has had an accident—nothing very serious, but he's in the emergency room getting some stitches in his head, and they want to drive down to Connecticut.

The phone rings. Michelle answers it, and after a brief exchange, hangs up and says to me, "Linda needs to borrow a car tonight... hers is in the garage again."

"Which Linda?" I say, as there are three: three close friends acquired since Garnet's death, all, amazingly, named Linda.

And I've just remembered that I was supposed to pick up a birthday cake for Angela, our friend from Brazil, who's coming over later for a celebration.

A while later, as I'm driving to the bakery with Sam, I recall the time, two years before, when we were riding together in this same car, down on Cape Cod, and Sam turned to me and said, "My arm is never going to grow, is it."

"No, sweetheart," I said. "I mean it'll get bigger, as you get bigger. But it'll always be the way it is now. Only bigger."

I had noticed, the moment before, his staring at me as I shifted the gears. After a pause, he said, "Darn. I won't ever be able to drive a car."

I laughed and said, "Of course you will, Sam. You won't have any trouble at all . . ." and then explained about automatic transmissions.

"Oh," he said when I was done. "Cool."

On the drive back home from the bakery, I recall a moment in Arkansas, at Garnet's wake: a red old man who turned out to be an uncle. He was very drunk, and at one point, united by our various needs for fresh air, we found ourselves shivering side by side on the front steps. We sat in the dark for what seemed a long time without speaking, and I noted the makes of the many gleaming automobiles parked on the road in front of the house. After a while, the man turned, looked at me as if he were sizing me up, shook his head, and looked straight ahead again. He said, "I hate every goddamned thing in this goddamned stinking world." Then he looked me in the eye, his face softening, and said, "But I loved Garnet." It was the extreme, black-and-white formulation of a drunk, but like many extreme, drunken formulations, it began at least in truth. There was honesty at its inception.

His face lingers in my mind all the way home, and as I pull into the driveway, I see that it's a liquor-ravaged version of the father's face I saw earlier in the restaurant, as the father gathered together his family's warm things, their hats and scarves and gloves, and said to me, "He's just so sick."

Now Michelle meets us at the door, on her way out, and clearly exasperated. "I forgot I was supposed to return these damned books I borrowed from Linda," she says. "She's leaving for Florida tonight and she's got to have them to take with her."

"Which Linda?" I say. Then, surprising her, I take her in my arms and kiss her. There's a flash of tension, having to do with time and place, and then I feel a familiar yielding of her body. I think of us lying prone on our big, barge-like bed upstairs, side by side, and my tracing with my finger the shoreline of the impressive little well at the small of her back—a spot I have named for a lake, the same name as her name.

"What?" she says when I release her.

"Nothing," I say. "Where's Katharine?"

"She's gone down to Sonia's for a while. They're working on something together for school. She's supposed to be back in half an hour."

In the kitchen, I put five candles on the cake. Angela, turning forty-four, is fully into the representative-candle stage of birthday cakes. I ask Sam to help me decide what each of the candles should stand for.

"Okay," he says without hesitation. "You write them down on the box."

I find a pen and poise it on the lid of the cakebox. For some reason, at that moment, I notice how tall and lean Sam has become, as handsome as ever, but his hair grown a bit long—(I make a mental note to get him to the barber)—and his front teeth suddenly very large and white. He appears to be caught in some flux between little boy and big boy.

"Okay," he says. "Are you ready?"

"Ready," I say.

"Okay. Love . . ."

I write, 1. *love.*

"Happiness . . ."

I write, 2. *happiness.*

"Sadness . . ."

"Are you sure?" I say. "A birthday wish?"

He gives me a resigned, impatient look—he knew I wouldn't be able to get through it without some tiny bit of questioning.

Nodding, I say, "Because sadness is a part of life, just like happiness and love?"

"Just write it," he says.

I write, 3. *sadness.*

Here he pauses, thinking, then says, "Forgiveness..."

I write, 4. *forgiveness.*

Another pause, then, "What's it called? Oh...and helpfulness. Is that the right word? Helpfulness. Is that what it's called?"

I tell him that's what it's called, and write it down.

PETER CAMERON, who works for the Lambda Legal Defense Fund in New York City, is the author of three short story collections: *One Way or Another, Leap Year, and Far-Flung Stories,* and of two novels, *The Weekend* and *Andorra.*

RON CARLSON is the author of three short story collections: *The News of the World, Plan B for the Middle Class,* and his newest, *The Hotel Eden: Stories,* and of a novel, *Betrayed by F. Scott Fitzgerald.* He lives in Scottsdale, Arizona.

ANGELA DAVIS-GARDNER, who wrote this piece even though two 300-foot oaks fell through her bedroom window in Raleigh, North Carolina during Hurricane Fran, is the author of the novels *Felice* and *Forms of Shelter,* and the forthcoming *The Woman.* Her next collection of short fiction is called *Fish Tales.*

TIM GAUTREAUX, a son of the South, is the author of the story collection *Same Place, Same Things.* He has won two National Magazine Awards and was recently named the John and Renee Grisham Southern Writer-in-Residence at the University of Mississippi. Gautreaux was born and raised in Louisiana, where he still resides.

MYRA GOLDBERG, who lives in New York City, is the author of *Whistling and Other Stories*, a 1993 *New York Times* Notable Book of the Year, and *Rosalind: A Family Romance*. She teaches at Sarah Lawrence College.

BRIAN HALL is the author of *The Saskiad*, a novel, and of *Madeleine's World: A Child's Journey from Birth to Age Three*. He lives with his wife and two young daughters in Ithaca, New York.

LINDA HOGAN, a Chickasaw poet, novelist, and essayist, lives in Idledale, Colorado. She is the author of *Mean Spirit* and *Solar Storms* (fiction), *Dwellings: Reflections on the Natural World* (essays), and *The Book of Medicines* and *Seeing Through the Sun* (poetry).

CAROLINE LEAVITT is the author of six novels: *Meeting Rozzy Halfway*, *Lifelines*, *Jealousies*, *Family*, *Into Thin Air*, and *Living Other Lives*. She lives in a 120-year-old rowhouse in Hoboken, New Jersey, with her husband, Jeff, their baby son Max, and their tortoise, Minnie.

MARGOT LIVESEY is the author of *Homework* and of *Criminals*, both novels, and of *Learning by Heart*, a collection of stories. She is a native of Scotland and lives in Cambridge, Massachusetts.

ELIZABETH MCCRACKEN'S first novel, about a librarian who falls in love with a young boy who can't stop growing, is *The Giant's House*. It was a finalist for the National Book Award in 1996. She also wrote the award-winning short story collection *Here's Your Hat, What's Your Hurry?* She lives in Somerville, Massachusetts.

DENNIS MCFARLAND, who also lives near Boston, with his wife and two children, is the author of *The Music Room, School for the Blind,* and most recently, *A Face at the Window,* the best ghost story that has been published in many years.

JOYCE CAROL OATES, for whom there are 75 entries on the computerized bibliography at the New York Public Library, is the Roger S. Berlind Distinguished Professor in the Humanities at Princeton University. She is the author of many novels, including *Marya: A Life, Because It Is Bitter, and Because It Is My Heart,* and *We Were the Mulvaneys.* Her short story collections include *Where Are You Going, Where Have You Been,* and *Heat: And Other Stories.* She is also a playwright (*Twelve Plays* and *In Darkest America,* among others) and a poet. She has written much nonfiction, including *On Boxing* and *(Woman) Writer: Occasions and Opportunities.* Her latest novel is *Man Crazy.*

LARRY O'CONNOR is the co-editor (with his wife, Mary Morris) of *Maiden Voyages: Writings of Women Travelers.* He is an editor for the special editions department of *The Wall Street Journal* and lives in Brooklyn, New York.

MICKEY PEARLMAN is the editor of seven anthologies, including *Between Friends* and *A Place Called Home,* and the co-author of *Tillie Olsen* and *A Voice of One's Own.* She is the author of *Listen to Their Voices: 20 Interviews with Women Who Write* and of *What to Read: The Essential Guide for Reading Group Members and Other Book Lovers,* now in a 10th printing. She lives in northern New Jersey.

CAROLYN SEE is the author of five novels: *The Rest Is Done with Mirrors; Mothers, Daughters; Rhine Maidens; Golden Days;* and *Making History;* of *Blue Money* (non-fiction), and a memoir: *Dreaming: Hard Luck and Good Times in America.* She is a book reviewer for *The Washington Post* and has a Ph.D. from UCLA, where she teaches English. She lives in Topanga Canyon, California.

KATHARINE WEBER, the author of *Objects in Mirror Are Closer Than They Appear,* a *New York Times* Notable Book of the Year, has recently been named one of *Granta's* "Best of Young American Novelists." She lives in Bethany, Connecticut with her husband and two daughters.

SHAWN WONG is the author of *Homebase,* winner of the Pacific Northwest Booksellers Award, and of *American Knees.* He is the editor of *Aiiieeeee! An Anthology of Asian American Writers* and *The Big Aiiieeeee! An Anthology of Chinese-American and Japanese-American Literature.* He is a professional drag racer and the chairman of the English Department at the University of Washington.